ON CHRISTIAN DYING
Classic and Contemporary Texts

Edited by
Matthew Levering

A SHEED & WARD BOOK
ROWMAN & LITTLEFIELD PUBLISHERS, INC.
Lanham • Boulder • New York • Toronto • Oxford

ON CHRISTIAN DYING
Classic and Contemporary Texts

Edited by
Matthew Levering

ROWMAN & LITTLEFIELD PUBLISHERS, INC.
Lanham • Boulder • New York • Toronto • Oxford

A SHEED & WARD BOOK

ROWMAN & LITTLEFIELD PUBLISHERS, INC.

Published in the United States of America
by Rowman & Littlefield Publishers, Inc.
A wholly owned subsidiary of the Rowman & Littlefield Publishing Group, Inc.
4501 Forbes Boulevard, Suite 200, Lanham, Maryland 20706
www.rowmanlittlefield.com

PO Box 317
Oxford
OX2 9RU, UK

Copyright © 2004 by Rowman & Littlefield Publishers, Inc.

All rights reserved. No part of this publication may be reproduced, stored
in a retrieval system, or transmitted in any form or by any means, electronic,
mechanical, photocopying, recording, or otherwise, without the prior permission
of the publisher.

British Library Cataloguing in Publication Information Available

Library of Congress Cataloging-in-Publication Data

On Christian dying : classic and contemporary texts / edited by Matthew Levering.
    p. cm.
  Includes bibliographical references and index.
  ISBN 0-7425-3464-2 (hardcover : alk. paper)—ISBN 0-7425-3465-0 (pbk. : alk. paper)
  1. Death—Religious aspects—Catholic Church. 2. Catholic Church—Doctrines.
I. Levering, Matthew Webb, 1971-
  BT825.O5 2004
  236'.1—dc22   2004005265

∞™ The paper used in this publication meets the minimum requirements of
American National Standard for Information Sciences—Permanence of Paper
for Printed Library Materials, ANSI/NISO Z39.48-1992.

In Memoriam

Eleanor Moretz Neumann, 1910–2004

And in tribute to her children

Lynn Moretz, Libby Wells, Virginia Hart, Joan Davis

Who beautifully assisted her Christian dying

Contents

Introduction	ix
St. Ignatius of Antioch	1
St. Polycarp of Smyrna	7
The Martyrs of Gaul	15
St. Anthanasius	27
St. Ambrose	33
St. Augustine	43
St. Thomas Aquinas	53
St. Catherine of Siena	65
St. Catherine of Genoa	73
St. Thomas More, Part I	79
St. Thomas More, Part II	89
St. John of the Cross	95
St. Francis de Sales	103
St. Joseph Cafasso	109
John Henry Newman	115
St. Therese of Lisieux	123
Index	133
About the Editor	137

Introduction

As a preparation for reading the saints' writings about death and dying, it is worthwhile to examine the insights of the great philosophers and poets. As Socrates remarked, "true philosophers make dying their profession, and . . . to them of all men death is least alarming."[1] In the *Phaedo*, Socrates teaches that "if a man has trained himself throughout his life to live in a state as close as possible to death, would it not be ridiculous for him to be distressed when death comes to him?"[2] In his view, philosophical purification or preparation for death "consists in separating the soul as much as possible from the body, and accustoming it to withdraw from all contact with the body and concentrate itself by itself, and to have its dwelling, so far as it can, both now and in the future, alone by itself, freed from the shackles of the body."[3]

Yet, can we be as unconcerned as Socrates about the loss of our bodily life? The poets suggest otherwise. For instance, the great English writer Samuel Johnson parodies Socratic philosophical calm in his novel *Rasselas*. Rasselas, the young protagonist of the novel, has set forth "to judge with my own eyes of the various conditions of men, and then to make deliberately my *choice of life*."[4] In his journeys, he stumbles across a professor of philosophy lecturing on how happiness flows from subduing the passions. Rasselas "fixed his eye upon a sage raised above the rest, who discoursed with great energy on the government of the passions. His look was venerable, his action graceful, his pronunciation clear, and his diction elegant." Persuaded that here he has found the path to a happy life, Rasselas resolves to apprentice himself to the philosopher and to imitate his life. He is warned, however, by his guide Imlac: "Be not too hasty," said Imlac, "to trust, or to admire, the teachers of morality: they discourse like angels, but they live like men."[5]

When Rasselas visits the philosopher a few days later, he is greeted by a broken man. Rasselas finds "the philosopher in a room half darkened, with his eyes misty, and his face pale. 'Sir, said he, you are come at a time when all human friendship is useless; what I suffer cannot be remedied, what I have lost cannot be supplied. My daughter, my only daughter, from whose tenderness I expected all the comforts of my age, died last night of a fever. My views, my purposes, my hopes are at an end.'"[6] Rasselas seeks to remind the philosopher that death should never surprise a wise man.

> "Young man," answered the philosopher, "you speak like one that has never felt the pangs of separation." "Have you then forgot the precepts," said Rasselas, "which you so powerfully enforced? Has wisdom no strength to arm the heart against calamity? Consider, that external things are naturally variable, but truth and reason are always the same." "What comfort," said the mourner, "can truth and reason afford me? of what effect are they now, but to tell me, that my daughter will not be restored?"[7]

Socrates remains calm in the face of his own death, but what about the grief of an old man for his only daughter? The anguish of death cannot be so easily dismissed.

Furthermore, even were philosophy a cure, few have the leisure or insight to be philosophers. Can philosophic exercises prepare poor people dying in the streets of Calcutta, for example? Are their deaths simply the last tragedy in lives that should never have been lived? In a television interview about her Home for the Dying, Mother Teresa told the British journalist Malcolm Muggeridge that "the first woman I saw I myself picked up from the street. She had been half eaten by the rats and ants. I took her to the hospital but they could not do anything for her."[8] Muggeridge then asks her to explain why she has chosen this way to help people. She responds,

> First of all we want to make them feel that they are wanted, we want them to know that there are people who really love them, who really

want them, at least for the few hours that they have to live, to know human and divine love. That they too may know that they are the children of God, and that they are not forgotten and that they are loved and cared about and there are young lives ready to give themselves in their service.[9]

Perhaps the true preparation that ennobles death consists in self-giving love that is enacted, with the dying person, by those who care for the dying. Death itself, in such a context, becomes a powerful act of sharing in love.

Does this view, however, romanticize the act of dying? Is it realistic? Again let us turn to the poets. In Walker Percy's brilliant novel *The Last Gentleman*, the protagonist, Will Barrett, has a teenage friend, Jamie Vaught, who is dying. Barrett finds the dying boy getting out of bed, and in helping put him back in bed he smells from Jamie's body "a foulness beyond the compass of smell. This could only be the dread ultimate rot of the molecules themselves, an abject surrender. It was the body's disgorgement of its most secret shame."[10] Barrett is deeply embarrassed for Jamie. It seems to him that Jamie has entered into an appalling state of humiliation. As Jamie begins to gurgle with the throes of approaching death, he accepts and receives baptism from a Catholic priest who has come at the request of Jamie's sister and brother. After Jamie has professed the faith with thickened tongue, his "bowels opened again with the spent schleppen sound of an old man's sphincter."[11] There is no time to get the bedpan, although Barrett tries to do so. After being baptized, Jamie asks for the priest to hold his hand until he is through dying. There is a deep ambiguity and chaotic sense of confusion and rapid loss. Yet, there is also the sense that these men—Jamie, the priest, Jamie's brother, and Will Barrett—are somehow participating in Jamie's giving of himself to God, a life-in-death. It is a profoundly noble and a profoundly humiliating moment all at once, much like what Mother Teresa describes.

Percy thus suggests that Mother Teresa's vision is true. In contrast, the novelist Aldous Huxley describes a culture that has lost the art of dying. In Huxley's *Brave New World*, the world has been divided into two parts. In the civilized portion of the world, extraordinary progress in empirical science, particularly in the areas of procreation, aging, and psychology, have created a civilization in which productivity, sexual promiscuity, and sports are the only recognized values. Armed with attractive Malthusian contraceptive cartridge belts, with a drug called *soma* that procures feelings of satisfaction and friendliness, with the music of "sexophones," and with packets of sex-hormone chewing gum, the men and women of this civilization spend their life under strict government regulations that prescribe time for working, for going to the Feelies (movies), for massages, for frequent and casual sexual relations, and for playing tennis and golf. The government's task is to ensure that there is "no leisure from pleasure, not a moment to sit down and think."[12] All books and signs of earlier civilizations—such as Christianity—have been obliterated. Solidarity Hymns, the sign of the T (for Model T automobiles), and worship of Ford, the great innovator of monochrome productivity and pleasure, have taken their place.

On a sightseeing vacation to a Savage Reservation, however, a civilized man mistakenly impregnates his friend Linda. When he wakes up she is gone and cannot be found. Linda remains among the savages, a drunken, aging, promiscuous woman, and raises her son. Eventually she and her son John, now a full-grown man, escape the Reservation. Upon her return to civilization, Linda turns completely to *soma*-induced pleasurable sleep, with doses large enough to cause death. She is taken to a Hospital for the Dying: "Linda was dying in company—in company with all the modern conveniences. The air was continuously alive with gay synthetic melodies. At the foot of every bed, confronting its moribund occupant, was a television box. Television was left on, a running tap, from morning till night. Every quarter of an hour the prevailing perfume of the room was automatically changed."[13]

When John—a savage who, unlike his mother, does not fit into this civilized world and who is filled with the poetry of Shakespeare—visits his mother, he shocks the nurse by his concern and dismay. Linda, however, is in her element. "Propped up on pillows, she was watching the Semi-finals of the South American Riemann-Surface Tennis Championship, which were being played in silent and diminished reproduction on the screen of the television box at the foot of the bed. . . . Her pale, bloated face wore an expression of imbecile happiness."[14] John tries to awaken her, tries to find some semblance of motherly recognition and love. When she does recognize him, however, she thinks of him solely as a boorish intruder into her *soma*-dream of remembered sexual pleasure.

Death comes for Linda suddenly, when the *soma* fatally cuts off her breathing: "She tried to cry out—but no sound came; only the terror of her staring eyes revealed what she was suffering. Her hands went to her throat, then clawed at the air. . . . The look she gave him was charged with an unspeakable terror—with terror and, it seemed to him, reproach. She tried to raise herself in bed, but fell back on the pillows. Her face was horribly distorted, her lips blue."[15] John rushes for a nurse, but Linda is already dead. Far from being concerned about Linda, the nurse is scandalized by John's display of grief in the presence of a group of young children. The nurse has charge of conditioning them not to fear the death of the individual but to care solely for society. As John grieves in anguish by his dead mother, the nurse wonders,

> Should she speak to him? try to bring him back to a sense of decency? remind him of where he was? of what fatal mischief he might do to these poor innocents? Undoing all their wholesome death-conditioning with this disgusting outcry—as though death were something terrible, as though any one mattered as much as all that! It might give them the most disastrous ideas about the subject, might upset them into reacting in the entirely wrong, the utterly anti-social way.[16]

In the end, she turns away and in a jolly tone offers the children chocolate eclairs by way of distracting their attention.

Such literary portrayals raise questions about our own dying. Will our death have meaning? Will we die in the company of friends? Will we receive the prayers and sacramental ministrations of a priest? Will we die alone in the nursing home, drugged and with the television on? Will we die young, embarrassed and humiliated by the unnatural decomposition of our body? Will we leave behind desperately grieving relatives who had depended upon us? How should we grieve for our loved ones who die before us? Are we prepared for death? Do we live our lives in such a way that they are a preparation for death? Can we live our lives in such a way as to prepare us for the event of death?

Such questions cry out for answers that go beyond the empirical. All too often, popular and influential analyses of dying rely solely upon what can be observed and measured clinically. Thus, the medical doctor Sherwin Nuland has described the biological processes by which we die, and the psychologist Elisabeth Kübler-Ross has described our emotional states as we come to grips with death. Their fundamentally impersonal analyses, however, cannot suffice when it comes to the radical particularity and importance of *our* death or the deaths of *our* loved ones.

When we read of strangers' deaths in the newspaper, whether in the mundane obituaries or in the large-scale horrific events covered on the front page, we often can speak abstractly and easily about death. Scandalized by the seemingly impersonal and unimportant character of such deaths, the literary critic George Steiner has argued that our culture cannot do justice to the personal experience of dying:

> Thus the sheer scale of death, its obscene technologies (some would say: "industrialization") and its namelessness have become paramount. ... Two contrasting yet congruent tendencies are at work. Where massacre and economic-social misery prevail, death withers to naked routine. No especial significance honours the victim, so often skeletal in his or her trashed existence. Where superfluity obtains, death is sanitized and gentrified. Medical care and technology—those tubes, those softly lit rooms—privilege the moribund party. At the same time, however, death is absorbed into an almost commercial process and sweet-and-sour uniformity.[17]

These words ring true about the deaths of people whom we do not know, and we may fear that they will turn out to be true, in others' minds, about our deaths. In fact Steiner goes so far in this direction as to argue, like the horribly misguided Kirilov in Dostoevsky's *The Devils*,[18] that our last foothold for securing a death that embodies a creative act of (autonomous) dignity is suicide. In Steiner's words, suicide is "the sole guarantor of privacy, of the autonomy of the self. Suicide is the critical act *par excellence*, the ironic dissent of the spirit from *kitsch*."[19] Once we see others' deaths as meaningless, the only way we can find our own death "meaningful" is to choose it ourselves; but in the very act of so choosing (and thus grasping at a self-imposed "meaning"), we thereby deny that our life has any *intrinsic* meaning. Like Kirilov, Steiner ignores the reality that destroying one's own life cannot be one's last "creative" act, because it is an act of radical negation.

The poet T. S. Eliot, who feared death, identifies the same situation—the numbing vastness of the number and monotony of the daily deaths of other human beings as opposed to the personal urgency of his own death—and arrives at a different solution. As opposed to suicide, he chooses to embrace "the dark" as a gift from the same source as that which gives life: "I said to my soul, be still, and let the dark come upon you/ Which shall be the darkness of God."[20] When death is understood as a letting-go into the hands of God, it has meaning. But this letting-go causes pain because it contrasts with our desire to be in control. In the same poem Eliot describes our fear

> Of belonging to another, or to others, or to God.
> The only wisdom we can hope to acquire
> Is the wisdom of humility: humility is endless.[21]

Henri Nouwen, writing shortly before his own death, suggests that this posture of humility is possible through faith. Just as the trapeze artist must completely let go so as to be properly caught by her partner, so also we must, in dying, completely let go in trusting and self-giving love so as to be "caught up" and embraced by the self-giving God revealed in Jesus Christ.[22]

For the Christian, to die is to be fully caught up in gift. But how can we learn to give this gift, to become people whose minds and hearts are attuned to the gift-character of existence, and thus to the reality of the Giver? The present volume explores how Christian saints have taught the art of dying. Christians believe that if in dying we bear the self-giving image of Christ's perfect love, we shall rise with him in his image. St. Paul delivers this *good news* of the crucified Lord to the Corinthians:

> Just as we have borne the image of the man of dust, we shall also bear the image of the man of heaven. . . . Lo! I tell you a mystery. We shall not all sleep, but we shall all be changed, in a moment, in the twinkling of an eye, at the last trumpet. For the trumpet will sound, and the dead will be raised imperishable, and we shall be changed. . . . [T]hen shall come to pass the saying that is written: "Death is swallowed up in victory." "O death, where is thy victory? O death, where is thy sting?" (1 Corinthians 15:49–55).[23]

Christ himself teaches the same thing: we must lose our lives in order to find them in God. Christ's death, as a self-giving sacrifice, reversed the first man and woman's selfish attempt at autonomous self-preservation apart from God. In dying, we, too, must be converted from selfishness to self-giving. In our selfishness, we imagine that we can cling to life and its pleasures as if we ourselves were its autonomous source. In fact, we must learn to imitate the self-giving love of the one who is perfect Gift, God himself. As Jesus says, "If any man would come after me, let him deny himself and take up his cross and follow me. For whoever would save his life will lose it, and whoever loses his life for my sake will find it" (Matthew 16:24–25).

Is this not, however, easier said than done? Can even the Christian believer accomplish this? Although the great fourth-century bishop St. Athanasius, for instance, rightly rejoiced in the Christians' willingness to accept martyrdom, nonetheless many Christians renounced their faith in the face of the Roman Empire's threats, and Christians throughout the centuries have been hardly immune from anxiety and fear of death. Certainly, the grace to conform our lives to Christ's sacrificial self-giving does not mean that these fears will necessarily be taken away. Jesus, knowing that he has the power to raise Lazarus from the dead, weeps when he comes to Lazarus's tomb (John 11:35). Death is the opposite of what God intends for his creatures. It is no wonder that Jesus weeps at this terrible deprivation. Likewise, in the garden of Gethsemane, Jesus, who has already foretold his death, sweats in agony as he prays for the cup to pass if it be God's will (Luke 22:44), and an angel comes to strengthen him.

The detachment from self—the humbling position of receiving everything and having ultimate governance of nothing—is a gift that we must learn to receive from our Creator. In contrast to sentimental depictions of Christianity, T. S. Eliot expresses the gaining of this detachment as a purgative "flame" or "torment" in which we, in our selfishness, are *opened* to God's self-giving Love: "Who then devised the torment? Love."[24] As Eliot goes on to say, therefore, "[w]e die with the dying" and are born again with them.[25] Those who die well, teach us how to live. By sharing in their dying, we learn how to live the self-giving movement that death requires of us. Witnessing to self-giving love, friends of the dying person strengthen the dying person's ability to surrender to God in self-giving love, that is, to learn the art of receiving all from the Giver and giving all in imitation of him.

One final example from the poets will assist us. The reality that the dying teach us how to live is at the core of Dostoevsky's *The Brothers Karamazov*. The theme appears most famously in Alyosha Karamazov's speech at the funeral of Ilyusha, a little boy (and figure of Christ) whom Alyosha had befriended. Alyosha urges the boys who are listening to him—and whose unjust persecutions, for which they had repented, had caused Ilyusha's death—to remember this moment:

> [E]ven if only one good memory remains with us in our hearts, that alone may serve some day for our salvation. Perhaps we will even become wicked later on, will even be unable to resist a bad action, will laugh at people's tears and at those who say, as Kolya exclaimed today: "I want to suffer for all people"—perhaps we will scoff wickedly at such people. And yet, no matter how wicked we may be—and God preserve us from it—as soon as we remember how we buried Ilyusha, how we loved him in his last days, and how we've been talking just now, so much as friends, so together, by this stone, the most cruel and jeering man among us, if we should become so, will still not dare laugh within himself at how kind and good he was at this present moment! Moreover, perhaps just this memory alone will keep him from great evil.[26]

If the dying teach us how to live (by modeling self-giving for us), then it will be by remembering such deaths that we learn gradually how to die to ourselves, how to lose our own lives so that we might (in love) save our lives.

The texts in *On Christian Dying* enable us to learn from the great Christian witnesses to the art of dying. In order to convey a sense of the two millennia of the Christian tradition, the volume begins with the early martyrs who died for their public profession of the Christian faith: St. Ignatius of Antioch, St. Polycarp of Smyrna, and the second-century martyrs of Gaul. These texts remind us that imitation of Christ has often meant grim persecution and willingness to die for Christ's name. As the risen Lord warned Peter, "Truly, truly, I say to you, when you were young, you girded yourself and walked where you would; but when you are old, you will stretch out your hands, and another will gird you and carry you where you do not wish to go. (This he said to show by what death he was to glorify God.) And after this he said to him, 'Follow me'" (John 21:18–19). As Roman soldiers are leading him in chains from Antioch (in modern-day Syria) to the Coliseum in Rome to be eaten alive by wild beasts as a warning to other Christians, St. Ignatius, bishop of Antioch, rejoices that Christ has enabled him to "follow" Christ by such a death, thereby witnessing to faith in the ultimate triumph of divine love. St. Polycarp, too, who as bishop of Smyrna knew both the evangelist John and St. Ignatius of Antioch, willingly undergoes martyrdom in his old age as a testimony to his faith and hope in Christ, in whom all will be resurrected and judged. In the persecutions in Gaul in the late second century, similarly, average Christians sacrifice everything rather than deny their God.

There next follow texts from the Patristic period (third century to the eighth century). In the fourth century, St. Athanasius, bishop of Alexandria and a great defender of Christian faith, wrote a biographical sketch of the extraordinary hermit St. Anthony. The peacefulness of St. Anthony's death comes from a lifetime of detaching himself from earthly goods so as to be united in mind and heart to God in Christ. Yet, St. Anthony's detachment does not mean that he no longer cares for the world; on the contrary, his union with God enables him to love each human being as a creature made in the image of God and destined for union in holiness with the Trinity. In contrast to St. Anthony's humble submission to death, we find the impassioned and grief-stricken eulogy offered by St. Ambrose, the fourth-century bishop of Milan, to his brother Satyrus. St. Anthony teaches us how to embrace death; St. Ambrose teaches us how to mourn the dead. From this same period, St. Augustine meditates upon the peaceful death of his beloved mother Monica, and his own turbulent emotions. On the one hand, he knows in faith that she is alive and with the Lord; on the other hand, he misses her profoundly.

The texts from the medieval period (eighth century to fifteenth century) emphasize the centrality of Christian simplicity as a means of imitation of Christ and preparation for death. As Jesus says, "No one can serve two masters; either he will hate the one and love the other, or he will be devoted to the one and despise the other. You cannot serve God and mammon" (Matthew 6:24). With scholastic precision, St. Thomas Aquinas depicts the radical simplicity of Christian martyrdom, which differs from some modern interreligious understandings of the "martyr" as a man of violence. St. Catherine of Siena presents poverty as the key to dying: those who are not attached to the things of this world (foolishly and idolatrously cleaving to creatures rather than to the Creator) will be able to enact the self-giving love that embodies Christ-like dying, a dying that in fact is true life. The only lasting thing toward which we can direct our minds and hearts is God himself. Finally, St. Catherine of Genoa, a married laywoman, in her excruciating and lengthy dying, shows us the nobility that can be present precisely in the humiliation of dying.

From the Reformation and early Modern period (fifteenth century to eighteenth century), we draw wisdom for dying from St. Thomas More, who, in preparing for his martyrdom by King Henry VIII, meditates upon Christ's agony in the Garden of Gethsemane in light of the sorrow that naturally accompanies the approach of bodily death. As Christ himself makes clear, Christians need not deny this profound sorrow as they approach their own death. St. Thomas More explains the same reality in a more personal way, in one of his last letters to his beloved daughter Margaret. Likewise, St. John of the Cross, the great Spanish mystical theologian and monk, explores the "dying" to self that the soul, in contemplative prayer, experiences. This profound desire for union with God, in the "darkness" of prayer, is already an experience of Christian dying. In this spirit, St. Francis de Sales, in a letter to St. Jane of Chantal upon the death of his youngest sister (who was staying with Jane of Chantal at the time), describes both the deep grieving of his family and their desire to abandon themselves completely to the providential will of God and trust entirely in God's plans for them.

Finally, from the Modern period, St. Joseph Cafasso, who lived in the nineteenth century and became revered for his ministry to convicts condemned to death, provides a prayer that expresses (as his preparation for his own death) the self-gift that we are called upon to give as the fundamental act of our life. Blessed John Henry Newman, the great English theologian, offers a sermon that calls upon his hearers to live with their future death in view, rather than to ignore and suppress the reality of dying. It is only by acknowledging daily that we are going to die, that we can live with eternal realities—Love—as our primary focus. The collection concludes with St. Therese of Lisieux, who inspires us to hope for the consolations that God gives to the dying person who perseveres in faith.

Thus, by learning how Christians have grieved, prayed, and died in Christ, we can come to imitate more and more powerfully their witness to self-giving love. These great Christians become our teachers in the art of dying, and we learn how to give up our own lives for Christ, and how to desire God and to trust completely in God even in the depths of our profound mourning for loved ones. By meditating upon these excerpts from the great saints and teachers of the Christian tradition, may we be strengthened in mind and heart in our ongoing "training," in Socrates's phrase, "to live in a state as close as possible to death"—that is, to live according to Christ's Cross.

St. Paul powerfully and repeatedly describes this cruciform mode of living. Let us therefore conclude with his words, written for those who seek, from Christian wisdom, to learn how to live by dying to self.

"I have been crucified with Christ; it is no longer I who live, but Christ who lives in me; and the life I now live in the flesh I live by faith in the Son of God, who loved me and gave himself for me" (Galatians 2:20).

"Do you not know that all of us who have been baptized into Christ Jesus were baptized into his death? . . . But if we have died with Christ, we believe that we shall also live with him" (Romans 6:3,8).

"None of us lives to himself, and none of us dies to himself. If we live, we live to the Lord, and if we die, we die to the Lord; so then, whether we live or whether we die, we are the Lord's" (Romans 14:8).

"We are treated as imposters, and yet are true; as unknown, and yet well known; as dying, and behold we live; as punished, and not yet killed; as sorrowful, yet always rejoicing; as poor, yet making many rich; as having nothing, yet possessing everything" (2 Corinthians 6:8–10).

"For to me to live is Christ, and to die is gain" (Philippians 1:21).

"For now we see in a mirror dimly, but then face to face. Now I know in part; then I shall understand fully, even as I have been fully understood. So faith, hope, love abide, these three; but the greatest of these is love" (1 Corinthians 13:12–13).

Notes

1. Plato, *Phaedo*, trans. Hugh Tredennick, in *The Collected Dialogues of Plato*, ed. Edith Hamilton and Huntington Cairns (Princeton: Princeton University Press, 1961): 67e (p. 50).
2. Plato, *Phaedo*, 67d and e.
3. Ibid., 67c and d.
4. Samuel Johnson, *Rasselas* (New York: Penguin Books, 1976 [1759]): 69.
5. Ibid., 80.
6. Ibid., 81.
7. Ibid.
8. Malcolm Muggeridge, *Something Beautiful for God: Mother Teresa of Calcutta* (San Francisco: Harper & Row, 1971): 91.

9. Ibid., 91–92.

10. Walker Percy, *The Last Gentleman* (New York: Ballantine Books, 1989 [1966]): 316.

11. Ibid., 319.

12. Aldous Huxley, *Brave New World* (New York: Harper & Row, 1989 [1932]): 55.

13. Ibid., 203.

14. Ibid., 204–205.

15. Ibid., 210–211.

16. Ibid., 211–212.

17. George Steiner, *Grammars of Creation* (New Haven, CT: Yale University Press, 2001): 324.

18. Fyodor Dostoevsky, *The Devils*, trans. David Magarshack (New York: Penguin Books, 1971): 566, 586–587, 605–621.

19. Steiner, 325.

20. T. S. Eliot, *Four Quartets* (New York: Harcourt Brace Jovanovich, 1988 [1943]): East Coker, 27.

21. Ibid., 26–27.

22. Henri J. M. Nouwen, *Our Greatest Gift: A Meditation on Dying and Caring* (New York: HarperSanFrancisco, 1994): 66–67.

23. St. Paul is quoting Isaiah 25:8 and Hosea 13:14.

24. T. S. Eliot, *Four Quartets*, Little Gidding, 57.

25. Ibid., 58.

26. Fyodor Dostoevsky, *The Brothers Karamazov*, trans. Richard Pevear and Larissa Volokhonsky (San Francisco: North Point Press, 1990): 774–775.

St. Ignatius of Antioch

St. Ignatius, Bishop of Antioch, wrote this letter to the Church in Rome as he was approaching Rome in chains around A.D. 110. Christianity was outlawed in the Roman Empire. Roman soldiers were leading him to martyrdom in the Coliseum, where he would be torn to shreds by wild animals before a crowd of spectators. Nonetheless, Ignatius begs the Church in Rome not to try to stop his martyrdom. He rejoices in his upcoming opportunity to witness to Christ's truth and love by giving his own life for God, and thereby to be perfectly configured to Christ's self-giving. He exemplifies the reality that true life is none other than life in God.

IGNATIUS, ALSO CALLED THEOPHORUS, to the Church that has found mercy in the transcendent Majesty of the Most High Father and of Jesus Christ, His only Son; the church by the will of Him who willed all things that exist, beloved and illuminated through the faith and love of Jesus Christ our God; which also presides in the chief place of the Roman territory; a church worthy of God, worthy of honor, worthy of felicitation, worthy of praise, worthy of success, worthy of sanctification, and presid-

Excerpts from *The Epistles of St. Clement of Rome and St. Ignatius of Antioch*, pp. 80–84, translated and annotated by James A. Kleist, S.J., Ph.D., from *Ancient Christian Writers*, Vol. 1, Copyright © 1946 by Rev. Johannes Quasten and Rev. Joseph C. Plumpe, Paulist Press, Inc., New York / Mahwah, NJ. Used with permission of Paulist Press, www.paulistpress.com.

ing love, maintaining the law of Christ, and bearer of the Father's name: her do I therefore salute in the name of Jesus Christ, the Son of the Father. Heartiest good wishes for unimpaired joy in Jesus Christ our God, to those who are united in flesh and spirit by every commandment of His; who imperturbably enjoy the full measure of God's grace and have every foreign stain filtered out of them.

By prayer to God I have obtained the favor of seeing your venerable faces; in fact, I have been pleading for an even greater favor: as a prisoner in Christ Jesus I hope to embrace you, provided it is His will that I should be privileged to reach the goal. An auspicious beginning has certainly been made—if only I obtain the grace of taking due possession of my inheritance without hindrance. The truth is, I am afraid it is your love that will do me wrong. For you, of course, it is easy to achieve your object; but for me it is difficult to win my way to God, should you be wanting in consideration for me.

Surely, I do not want you *to court the good pleasure of men*, but to please God, as indeed you do please Him. Yes, I shall never again have such an opportunity of winning my way to God, nor can you, if you remain quiet, ever have your name inscribed on a more glorious achievement. For, if you quietly ignore me, I am the word of God; but if you fall in love with my human nature, I shall, on the contrary, be a mere sound. Grant me no more than that you let my blood be spilled in sacrifice to God, while yet there is an altar ready. You should form a choir of love and sing a song to the Father through Jesus Christ, because God has graciously summoned the bishop of Syria to come from the rising of the sun to the setting. How glorious to be a setting sun—away from the world, on to God! May I rise in His presence!

You have never grudged any man. You have taught others. All I want is that the lessons you inculcate in initiating disciples remain in force. Only beg for me strength within and without, that I may be a man not merely of words, but also of resolution. In this way I shall not only be called a Christian, but also prove to be one. For if I prove to be one, I can also be called a true believer even then when I am no longer seen by the world. Nothing that is seen is good. Our God Jesus Christ certainly is the more clearly seen now that He is in the Father. Whenever Christianity is hated by the world, what counts is not power of persuasion, but greatness.

I am writing to all the Churches and state emphatically to all that I die willingly for God, provided you do not interfere. I beg you, do not show me unseasonable kindness. Suffer me to be the food of wild beasts, which are the means of my making my way to God. God's wheat I am, and by the teeth of wild beasts I am to be ground that I may prove Christ's pure bread. Better still, coax the wild beasts to become my tomb and to leave no part of my person behind: once I have fallen asleep, I do not wish to be a burden to anyone. Then only shall I be a genuine disciple of Jesus Christ when the world will not see even my body. Petition Christ in my behalf that through these instruments I may prove God's sacrifice. Not like Peter and Paul do I issue any orders to you. They were Apostles, I am a convict; they were free, I am until this moment a slave. But once I have suffered, I shall become a freedman of Jesus Christ, and, united with Him, I shall rise a free man. Just now I learn, being in chains, to desire nothing.

All the way from Syria to Rome I am fighting wild beasts, on land and sea, by day and night, chained as I am to ten leopards, that is, a detachment of soldiers, who prove themselves the more malevolent for kindnesses shown them. Yet in the school of this abuse I am more and more trained in discipleship, *although I am not therefore justified.* Oh, may the beasts prepared for me be my joy! And I pray that they may be found to be ready for me. I will even coax them to make short work of me, not as has happened to some whom they were too timid to touch. And should they be unwilling to attack me who am willing, I will myself compel them. Pardon me—I know very well where my advantage lies. At last I am well on the way to be a disciple. May nothing, *seen or unseen,* fascinate me, so that I may happily make my way to Jesus Christ! Fire, cross, struggles with wild beasts, wrenching of bones, mangling of limbs, crunching of the whole body, cruel tortures inflicted by the devil—let them come upon me, provided only I make my way to Jesus Christ.

Of no use to me will be the farthest reaches of the universe or the kingdoms of this world. *I would rather die* and come to Jesus Christ than be king over the entire earth. Him I seek who died for us; Him I love who rose again because of us. The birth pangs are upon me. Forgive me, brethren; do not obstruct my coming to life—do not wish me to die; do not make a gift to the world of one who wants to be God's. Beware of seducing me with matter; suffer me to receive pure light. Once arrived there, I shall be a man. Permit me to be an imitator of my suffering God. If anyone holds Him in his heart, let him understand what I am aspiring to; and then let him sympathize with me, knowing in what distress I am.

The prince of this world is resolved to abduct me, and to corrupt my Godward aspirations. Let none of you, therefore, who will then be present, assist him. Rather, side with me, that is, with God. Do not have Jesus Christ on your lips, and the world in your hearts. Give envy no place among you. And should I upon my arrival plead for your intervention, do not listen to me. Rather, give heed to what I write to you. I am writing while still alive, but my yearning is for death. My Love has been crucified, and I am not on fire with the love of earthly things. But there is in me a *Living Water*, which is eloquent and within me says: "Come to the Father." I have no taste for corruptible food or for the delights of this life. *Bread of God* is what I desire; that is, the Flesh of Jesus Christ, *who was of the seed of David*; and for my drink I desire His Blood, that is, incorruptible love.

No longer do I wish to live after the manner of men; and this is what will happen if you wish it so. Wish it, that your own wishes, too, may be fulfilled. By this short letter I beseech you: do believe me! Jesus Christ will make it clear to you that I speak the truth—He on whose lips there are no lies, through whom the Father has spoken truthfully. Pray for me that I may succeed. What I write to you does not please the appetites of the flesh, but it pleases the mind of God. If I suffer, you have loved me; if I am rejected, you have hated me!

Remember in your prayers the Church in Syria, which now has God for her Shepherd in my stead. Jesus Christ alone will be her Bishop, together with your love. For myself, I am ashamed to be counted as one of her members. I certainly do not deserve to be one, being the least of them and one that came to birth unexpectedly. However, if I but make my way to God, then by His mercy I shall be someone. My spirit salutes you, and so does the affection of the Churches that offered their hospitality to me, not as to a chance visitor, but in deference to Jesus Christ. Why, even those not adjoining my route—the route by which my body traveled—hastened in advance from town after town to meet me.

I am sending you this letter from Smyrna through the kindness of the Ephesians, who deserve so much praise. Among many others Crocus is here with me—a dearly beloved name to me! As to the men from Syria who for the glory of God have gone to Rome to meet you there, you have, I trust, made their acquaintance. Please, inform them also that I am near. One and all they are men of God and will be an honor to you. You will do well to give them every comfort. I am writing this to you on the 24th of August. Farewell to the end of the patient endurance of Jesus Christ.

Questions for St. Ignatius of Antioch

1. Why does Ignatius ask the members of the Church in Rome not to petition on his behalf?
2. What should we make of his desire for conformity to Christ?
3. In preparing for death, how should we discipline our love of earthly things?

St. Polycarp of Smyrna

Bishop of Smyrna and friend of St. Ignatius of Antioch, St. Polycarp was martyred by Roman soldiers around A.D. 156, when he was eighty years old. The following excerpt comes from the account of the persecution in Smyrna sent to neighboring churches by the Church in Smyrna. Polycarp's decision to be burned alive rather than deny Christ, as well as the flames' inability to consume Polycarp's body, are presented as marks of his holiness. The dove that comes forth from Polycarp's heart is the symbol of the Holy Spirit, promised by Christ to every believer. The account emphasizes that when filled with the Holy Spirit, the dying of a Christian becomes like Christ's dying, a gift of self that embodies love for God and neighbor.

THE CHURCH OF GOD which sojourns at Smyrna, to the Church of God sojourning in Philomelium, and to all the congregations of the Holy and Catholic Church in every place: Mercy, peace, and love from God the Father, and our Lord Jesus Christ, be multiplied.

We have written to you, brethren, as to what relates to the martyrs, and especially to the blessed Polycarp, who put an end to the persecution, having, as it were, set a seal upon it by his martyrdom. For almost all the events that happened previously [to this one], took place that the

From: *Apostolic Fathers, Justin Martyr, Irenaeus,* Vol. 1 of *Ante-Nicene Fathers,* ed. and trans. Alexander Roberts and James Donaldson (Peabody, MA: Hendrickson, 1994), pp. 39–42.

Lord might show us from above a martyrdom becoming the Gospel. For he waited to be delivered up, even as the Lord had done, that we also might become his followers, while we look not merely at what concerns ourselves, but have regard also to our neighbors. For it is the part of a true and well-founded love, not only to wish one's self to be saved, but also all the brethren.

All the martyrdoms, then, were blessed and noble which took place according to the will of God. For it becomes us who profess greater piety than others, to ascribe the authority over all things to God. And truly, who can fail to admire their nobleness of mind, and their patience, with that love towards their Lord which they displayed?—who, when they were so torn with scourges, that the frame of their bodies, even to the very inward veins and arteries, was laid open, still patiently endured, while even those that stood by pitied and bewailed them. But they reached such a pitch of magnanimity, that not one of them let a sigh or a groan escape them; thus proving to us all that those holy martyrs of Christ, at the very time when they suffered such torments, were absent from the body, or rather, that the Lord then stood by them, and communed with them. And, looking to the grace of Christ, they despised all the torments of this world, redeeming themselves from eternal punishment by [the suffering of] a single hour. For this reason the fire of their savage executioners appeared cool to them. For they kept before their view escape from that fire which is eternal and never shall be quenched, and looked forward with the eyes of their heart to those good things which are laid up for such as endure; things "which ear hath not heard, nor eye seen, neither have entered into the heart of man," but were revealed by the Lord to them, inasmuch as they were no longer men, but had already become angels. And, in like manner, those who were condemned to the wild beasts endured dreadful tortures, being stretched out upon beds full of spikes, and subjected to various other kinds of torments, in order that, if it were possible, the tyrant might, by their lingering tortures, lead them to a denial [of Christ].

For the devil did indeed invent many things against them; but thanks be to God, he could not prevail over all. For the most noble Germanicus strengthened the timidity of others by his own patience, and fought heroically with the wild beasts. For, when the proconsul sought to persuade him, and urged him to take pity on his age, he attracted the wild beast towards himself, and provoked it, being desirous to escape all the more quickly from an unrighteous and impious world. But upon this the whole multitude, marveling at the nobility of mind displayed by the devout and godly race of Christians, cried out, "Away with the Atheists;[1] let Polycarp be sought out."

Now one named Quintus, a Phrygian, who was but lately come from Phrygia, when he saw the wild beasts, became afraid. This was the man who forced himself and some others to come forward voluntarily [for trial]. Him the proconsul, after many entreaties, persuaded to swear and to offer sacrifice. Wherefore, brethren, we do not commend those who give themselves up [to suffering], seeing the Gospel does not teach so to do.

But the most admirable Polycarp, when he first heard [that he was sought for], was in no measure disturbed, but resolved to continue in the city. However, in deference to the wish of many, he was persuaded to leave it. He departed, therefore, to a country house not far distant from the city. There he stayed with a few [friends], engaged in nothing else night and day than praying for all men, and for the Churches throughout the world, according to his usual custom. And while he was praying, a vision presented itself to him three days before he was taken; and, behold, the pillow under his head seemed to him on fire. Upon this, turning to those that were with him, he said to them prophetically, "I must be burnt alive."

And when those who sought for him were at hand, he departed to another dwelling, whither his pursuers immediately came after him. And when they found him not, they seized upon two youths [that were there], one of whom, being subjected to torture, confessed. It was thus impossible that he should continue hid, since those that betrayed him were of his own household. The Irenarch then (whose office is the same as that of the Cleronomus), by name Herod, hastened to bring him into the stadium. [This all happened] that he might fulfill his special lot, being made a partaker of Christ, and that they who betrayed him might undergo the punishment of Judas himself.

His pursuers then, along with horsemen, and taking the youth with them, went forth at suppertime on the day of the preparation, with their usual weapons, as if going out against a robber. And being come about evening [to the place where he was], they found him lying down in the upper room of a certain little house, from which he might have escaped into another place; but he refused, saying, "The will of God be done." So when he heard that they were come, he went down and spoke with them.

And as those that were present marveled at his age and constancy, some of them said, "Was so much effort made to capture such a venerable man?" Immediately then, in that very hour, he ordered that something to eat and drink should be set before them, as much indeed as they cared for, while he besought them to allow him an hour to pray without disturbance. And on their giving him leave, he stood and prayed, being full of the grace of God, so that he could not cease for two full hours, to the astonishment of them that heard him, insomuch that many began to repent that they had come forth against so godly and venerable an old man.

Now, as soon as he had ceased praying, having made mention of all that had at any time come in contact with him, both small and great, illustrious and obscure, as well as the whole Catholic Church throughout the world, the time of his departure having arrived, they set him upon an ass, and conducted him into the city, the day being that of the great Sabbath. And the Irenarch Heron, accompanied by his father Nicetes (both riding in a chariot), met him, and taking him up into the chariot, they seated themselves beside him, and endeavored to persuade him, saying, "What harm is there in saying, Lord Caesar, and in sacrificing with the other ceremonies observed on such occasions, and so make sure of safety?" But he at first gave them no answer; and when they continued to urge him, he said, "I shall not do as you advise me." So they, having no hope of persuading him, began to speak bitter words unto him, and cast him with violence out of the chariot, insomuch that, in getting down from the carriage, he dislocated his leg [by the fall]. But without being disturbed, and as if suffering nothing, he went eagerly forward with all haste, and was conducted to the stadium, where the tumult was so great, that there was no possibility of being heard.

Now, as Polycarp was entering into the stadium, there came to him a voice from heaven, saying, "Be strong, and show thyself a man, O Polycarp!" No one saw who it was that spoke to him; but those of our brethren who were present heard the voice. And as he was brought forward, the tumult became great when they heard that Polycarp was taken. And when he came near, the proconsul asked him whether he was Polycarp. On his confessing that he was, [the proconsul] sought go persuade him to deny [Christ], saying, "Have respect to thy old age," and other similar things, according to their custom, [such as], "Swear by the fortune of Caesar; repent, and say, Away with the Atheists." But Polycarp, gazing with a stern countenance on all the multitude of the wicked heathen then in the stadium, and waving his hand towards them, while with groans he looked up to heaven, said, "Away with the Atheists." Then, the proconsul urging him, and saying, "Swear, and I will set you at liberty, reproach Christ;" Polycarp declared, "Eighty and six years have I served Him, and He never did me any injury: how then can I blaspheme my King and my Savior?"

And when the proconsul yet again pressed him, and said, "Swear by the fortune of Caesar," he answered, "Since you are vainly urgent that, as you say, I should swear by the fortune of Caesar, and pretend not to know who and what I am, hear me declare with boldness, I am a Christian. And if you wish to learn what the doctrines of Christianity are, appoint me a day, and you shall hear them." The proconsul replied, "Persuade the people." But Polycarp said, "To you I have thought it right to offer an account [of my faith]; for we are taught to give all due honor (which entails no injury upon ourselves) to the powers and authorities which are ordained of God. But as for *these*, I did not deem them worthy of receiving any account from me."

The proconsul then said to him, "I have wild beasts at hand; to these will I cast you, unless you repent." But he answered, "Call them then, for we are not accustomed to repent of what is good in order to adopt that which is evil; and it is well for me to be changed from what is evil to what is righteous." But again the proconsul said to him, "I will cause you to be consumed by fire, seeing you despise the wild beasts, if you will not repent." But Polycarp said, "You threaten me with fire which burns for an hour, and after a little is extinguished, but are ignorant of the fire of the coming judgment and of eternal punishment reserved for the ungodly. But why do you wait? Bring forth what you will."

While he spoke these and many other like things, he was filled with confidence and joy and his countenance was full of grace, so that not merely did it not fall as if troubled by the things said to him, but, on the contrary, the proconsul was astonished, and sent his herald to proclaim in the midst of the stadium thrice, "Polycarp has confessed that he is a Christian." This proclamation having been made by the herald, the whole multitude both of the heathen and Jews, who dwelt at Smyrna, cried out with uncontrollable fury, and in a loud voice, "This is the teacher of Asia, the father of the Christians, and the overthrower of our gods, he who has been teaching many not to sacrifice, or to worship the gods." Speaking thus, they cried out, and besought Philip the Asiarch to let loose a lion upon Polycarp. But Philip answered that it was not lawful for him to do so, seeing the shows of wild beasts were already finished. Then it seemed good to them to cry out with one consent, that Polycarp should be burnt alive. For thus it behooved the vision which was revealed to him in regard to his pillow to be fulfilled, when, seeing it on fire as he was praying, he turned about and said prophetically to the faithful that were with him, "I must be burnt alive."

This, then, was carried into effect with greater speed than it was spoken, the multitudes immediately gathering together wood and fagots out of the shops and baths; the Jews especially, according to custom, eagerly assisting them in it. And when the funeral pile was ready, Polycarp, laying aside all his garments, and loosing his girdle, sought also to take off his sandals—a thing he was not accustomed to do, inasmuch as every one of the faithful was always eager who should first touch his skin. For, on account of his holy life, he was, even before his martyrdom, adorned with every kind of good. Immediately then they surrounded him with those substances which had been prepared for the funeral pile. But when they were about also to fix him with nails, he said, "Leave me as I am; for He that gives me strength to endure the fire, will also enable me, without your securing me by nails, to remain without moving in the pile."

They did not nail him then, but simply bound him. And he, placing his hands behind him, and being bound like a distinguished ram [taken] out of a great flock for sacrifice, and prepared to be an acceptable burnt-offering unto God, looked up to heaven, and said, "O Lord God Almighty, the Father of Your beloved and blessed Son Jesus Christ, by whom we have received the knowledge of You, the God of angels and powers, and of every creature, and of the whole race of the righteous who live before you, I give You thanks that You have counted me worthy of this day and this hour, that I should have a part in the number of Your martyrs, in the cup of thy Christ, to the resurrection of eternal life, both of soul and body, through the incorruption [imparted] by the Holy Ghost. Among whom may I be accepted this day before You as a fat and acceptable sacrifice, according as You, the ever-truthful God, have foreordained, have revealed beforehand to me, and now have fulfilled. Wherefore also I praise You for all things, I bless You, I glorify You, along with the everlasting and heavenly Jesus Christ, Your beloved Son, with whom, to You, and the Holy Spirit, be glory both now and to all coming ages. Amen."

When he had pronounced this *amen*, and so finished his prayer, those who were appointed for the purpose kindled the fire. And as the flame blazed forth in great fury, we, to whom it was given to witness it, beheld a great miracle, and have been preserved that we might report to others what then took place. For the fire, shaping itself into the form of an arch, like the sail of a ship when filled with the wind, encompassed as by a circle the body of the martyr. And he appeared within not like flesh which is burnt, but as bread that is baked, or as gold and silver glowing in a furnace. Moreover, we perceived such a sweet odor [coming from the pile], as if frankincense or some such precious spices had been smoking there.

At length, when those wicked men perceived that his body could not be consumed by the fire, they commanded an executioner to go near and pierce him through with a dagger. And on his doing this, there came forth a dove, and a great quantity of blood, so that the fire was extinguished; and all the people wondered that there should be such a difference between the unbelievers and the elect, of whom this most admirable Polycarp was one, having in our own times been an apostolic and prophetic teacher, and bishop of the Catholic Church which is in Smyrna. For every word that went out of his mouth either has been or shall yet be accomplished.

Questions for St. Polycarp of Smyrna

1. If faced with the trial of martyrdom, would we stand with Germanicus or with Quintus?
2. Meditate upon Polycarp's prayer as he was facing being burned alive.
3. What is the content of "holiness" as described in this text, and what can such an understanding of holiness teach us about dying?

Notes

1. Christians were called "atheists" because they refused to worship the gods.

The Martyrs of Gaul

The fourth-century historian of the early Church, Bishop Eusebius of Caesarea, included this account of the second-century martyrs of Gaul in his *Church History*. In the striking depictions of human beings compelled by military power either to reject their faith or to suffer death as a punishment, we are reminded once again that many have considered their relationship with Christ to be worth dying for. Even if we die at a ripe old age in our beds, the martyrs remind us that in order to learn to die well, we must learn to choose God above any created reality, which will always be difficult in our fallen state. True martyrdom endures violence but is not, in contrast to suicide, a violent act.

OTHER WRITERS OF HISTORY RECORD THE VICTORIES of war and trophies won from enemies, the skill of generals, and the manly bravery of soldiers, defiled with blood and with innumerable slaughters for the sake of children and country and other possessions. But our narrative of the government of God will record in ineffaceable letters the most peaceful wars waged in behalf of the peace of the soul, and will tell of men doing brave deeds for truth rather than country, and for piety rather than dearest friends. It will hand down to imperishable remembrance the discipline

From: *Eusebius: Church History, Life of Constantine the Great, Oration in Praise of Constantine*, Vol. 1 of *Nicene and Post-Nicene Fathers*, ed. Philip Schaff (Peabody, MA: Hendrickson, 1994), trans. Arthur McGiffert, pp. 211–218.

and the much-tried fortitude of the athletes of religion, the trophies won from demons, the victories over invisible enemies, and the crowns placed upon all their heads.

The country in which the arena was prepared for them was Gaul, of which Lyons and Vienne are the principal and most celebrated cities. The Rhone passes through both of them, flowing in a broad stream through the entire region. The most celebrated churches in that country sent an account of the witnesses to the churches in Asia and Phrygia, relating in the following manner what was done among them. I will give their own words.

"The servants of Christ residing at Vienne and Lyons, in Gaul, to the brethren throughout Asia and Phrygia, who hold the same faith and hope of redemption, peace and grace and glory from God the Father and Christ Jesus our Lord."

Then, having related some other matters, they begin their account in this manner: "The greatness of the tribulation in this region, and the fury of the heathen against the saints, and the sufferings of the blessed witnesses, we cannot recount accurately, nor indeed could they possibly be recorded. For with all his might the adversary fell upon us, giving us a foretaste of his unbridled activity at his future coming. He endeavored in every manner to practice and exercise his servants against the servants of God, not only shutting us out from houses and baths and markets, but forbidding any of us to be seen in any place whatever. But the grace of God led the conflict against him, and delivered the weak, and set them as firm pillars, able through patience to endure all the wrath of the Evil One. And they joined battle with him, undergoing all kinds of shame and injury; and regarding their great sufferings as little, they hastened to Christ, manifesting truly that 'the sufferings of this present time are not worthy to be compared with the glory which shall be revealed to us.' First of all, they endured nobly the injuries heaped upon them by the populace; clamors and blows and draggings and robberies and stonings and imprisonments, and all things which an infuriated mob delights in inflicting on enemies and adversaries. Then, being taken to the forum by the chiliarch and the authorities of the city, they were examined in the presence of the whole multitude, and having confessed, they were imprisoned until the arrival of the governor. When, afterwards, they were brought before him, and he treated us with the utmost cruelty, Vettius Epagathus, one of the brethren, and a man filled with love for God and his neighbor, interfered. His life was so consistent that, although young, he had attained a reputation equal to that of the elder Zacharias: for he walked in all the commandments and ordinances of the Lord blameless, and was untiring in every good work for his neighbor, zealous for God and fervent in spirit. Such being his character, he could not endure the unreasonable judgment against us, but was filled with indignation, and asked to be permitted to testify in behalf of his brethren, that there is among us nothing ungodly or impious. But those about the judgment seat cried out against him, for he was a man of distinction; and the governor refused to grant his just request, and merely asked if he were also a Christian. And he, confessing this with a loud voice, was himself taken into the order of the witnesses, being called the Advocate of the Christians, but having the Advocate in himself, the Spirit more abundantly than Zacharias. He showed this by the fullness of his love, being well pleased even to lay down his life in defense of the brethren. For he was and is a true disciple of Christ, 'following the Lamb whithersoever he goes.'

"Then the others were divided, and the proto-witnesses were manifestly ready, and finished their confession with all eagerness. But some appeared unprepared and untrained, weak as yet, and unable to endure so great a conflict. About ten of these proved abortions, causing us great grief and sorrow beyond measure, and impairing the zeal of the others who had not yet been seized, but who, though suffering all kinds of affliction, continued constantly with the witnesses and did not forsake them. Then all of us feared greatly on account of uncertainty as to their confession; not because we dreaded the sufferings to be endured, but because we looked to the end, and were afraid that some of them might fall away. But those who were worthy were seized day by day, filling up their number, so that all the zealous persons, and those through whom especially our affairs had been established, were collected together out of the two churches. And some of our heathen servants also were seized, as the governor had commanded that all of us should be examined publicly. These, being ensnared by Satan, and fearing for themselves the tortures which they beheld the saints endure, and being also urged on by the soldiers, accused us falsely of Thyestean banquets and Oedipodean intercourse, and of deeds which are not only unlawful for us to speak of or to think, but which we cannot believe were ever done by men. When these accusations were reported, all the people raged like wild beasts against us, so that even if any had before been moderate on account of friendship, they were now exceedingly furious and gnashed their teeth against us. And that which was spoken by our Lord was fulfilled: 'The time will come when whosoever kills you will think that he does God service.' Then finally the holy witnesses endured sufferings beyond description, Satan striving earnestly that some of the slanders might be uttered by them also.

"But the whole wrath of the populace, and governor, and soldiers was aroused exceedingly against Sanctus, the deacon from Vienne, and Maturus, a late convert, yet a noble combatant, and against Attalus, a native of Pergamos, where he had always been a pillar and foundation, and Blandina, through whom Christ showed that things which appear mean and obscure and despicable to men are with God of great glory, through love toward him manifested in power, and not boasting in appearance. For while we all trembled, and her earthly mistress, who was herself also one of the witnesses, feared that on account of the weakness of her body, she would be unable to make bold confession, Blandina was filled with such power as to be delivered and raised above those who were torturing her by turns from morning till evening in every manner, so that they acknowledged that they were conquered, and could do nothing more to her. And they were astonished at her endurance, as her entire body was mangled and broken; and they testified that one of these forms of torture was sufficient to destroy life, not to speak of so many and so great sufferings. But the blessed woman, like a noble athlete, renewed her strength in her confession; and her comfort and recreation and relief from the pain of her sufferings was in exclaiming, 'I am a Christian and there is nothing vile done by us.'

"But Sanctus also endured marvelously and superhumanly all the outrages which he suffered. While the wicked men hoped, by the continuance and severity of his tortures to wring something from him which he ought not to say, he girded himself against them with such firmness that he would not even tell his name, or the nation or city to which he belonged, or whether he was bond or free, but answered in the Roman tongue to all their questions, 'I am a Christian.' He confessed this instead of name and city and race and everything besides, and the people heard from him no other word. There arose therefore on the part of the governor and his tormentors a great desire to conquer him; but having nothing more that they could do to him, they finally fastened red-hot brazen plates to the most tender parts of his body. And these indeed were burned, but he continued unbending and unyielding, firm in his confession, and refreshed and strengthened by the heavenly fountain of the water of life, flowing from the bowels of Christ. And his body was a witness of his sufferings, being one complete wound and bruise, drawn out of shape, and altogether unlike a human form. Christ, suffering in him, manifested his glory, delivering him from his adversary, and making him an example for the others, showing that nothing is fearful where the love of the Father is, and nothing painful where there is the glory of Christ. For when the wicked men tortured him a second time after some days, supposing that with his body swollen and inflamed to such a degree that he could not bear the touch of a hand, if they should again apply the same instruments, they would overcome him, or at least by his death under his sufferings others would be made afraid, not only did not this occur, but, contrary to all human expectation, his body arose and stood erect in the midst of the subsequent torments, and resumed its original appearance and the use of its limbs, so that, through the grace of Christ, these second sufferings became to him, not torture, but healing.

"But the devil, thinking that he had already consumed Biblias, who was one of those who had denied Christ, desiring to increase her condemnation through the utterance of blasphemy, brought her again to the torture, to compel her, as already feeble and weak, to report impious things concerning us. But she recovered herself under the suffering, and as if awaking from a deep sleep, and reminded by the present anguish of the eternal punishment in hell, she contradicted the blasphemers. 'How,' she said, 'could those eat children who do not think it lawful to taste the blood even of irrational animals?' And thenceforward she confessed herself a Christian, and was given a place in the order of the witnesses.

"But as the tyrannical tortures were made by Christ of no effect through the patience of the blessed, the devil invented other contrivances—confinement in the dark and most loathsome parts of the prison, stretching of the feet to the fifth hole in the stocks, and the other outrages which his servants are accustomed to inflict upon the prisoners when furious and filled with the devil. A great many were suffocated in prison, being chosen by the Lord for this manner of death, that he might manifest in them his glory. For some, though they had been tortured so cruelly that it seemed impossible that they could live, even with the most careful nursing, yet, destitute of human attention, remained in the prison, being strengthened by the Lord, and invigorated both in body and soul; and they exhorted and encouraged the rest. But such as were young, and arrested recently, so that their bodies had not become accustomed to torture, were unable to endure the severity of their confinement, and died in prison.

"The blessed Pothinus, who had been entrusted with the bishopric of Lyons, was dragged to the judgment seat. He was more than ninety years of age, and very infirm, scarcely indeed able to breathe because of physical weakness; but he was strengthened by spiritual seal through his earnest desire for martyrdom. Though his body was worn out by old age and disease, his life was preserved that Christ might triumph in it. When he was brought by the soldiers to the tribunal, accompanied by the civil magistrates and a multitude who shouted against him in every manner as if he were Christ himself, he bore noble witness. Being asked by the governor, Who was the God of the Christians, he replied, 'If you are worthy, you shall know.' Then he was dragged away harshly, and received blows of every kind. Those near him struck him with their hands and feet, regardless of his age; and those at a distance hurled at him whatever they could seize; all of them thinking that they would be guilty of great wickedness and impiety if any possible abuse were omitted. For thus they thought to avenge their own deities. Scarcely able to breathe, he was cast into prison and died after two days.

"Then a certain great dispensation of God occurred, and the compassion of Jesus appeared beyond measure, in a manner rarely seen among the brotherhood, but not beyond the power of Christ. For those who had recanted at their first arrest were imprisoned with the others, and endured terrible sufferings, so that their denial was of no profit to them even for the present. But those who confessed what they were, were imprisoned as Christians, no other accusation being brought against them. But the first were treated afterwards as murderers and defiled, and were punished twice as severely as the others. For the joy of martyrdom, and the hope of the promises, and love for Christ, and the Spirit of the Father supported the latter; but their consciences so greatly distressed the former that they were easily distinguishable from all the rest by their very countenances when they were led forth. For the first went out rejoicing, glory and grace being blended in their faces, so that even their bonds seemed like beautiful ornaments, as those of a bride adorned with variegated golden fringes; and they were perfumed with the sweet savor of Christ, so that some supposed they had been anointed with earthly ointment. But the others were downcast and humble and dejected and filled with every kind of disgrace, and they were reproached by the heathen as ignoble and weak, bearing the accusation of murderers, and having lost the one honorable and glorious and life-giving Name. The rest, beholding this, were strengthened, and when apprehended, they confessed without hesitation, paying no attention to the persuasions of the devil."

After certain other words they continue: "After these things, finally, their martyrdoms were divided into every form. For plaiting a crown of various colors and of all kinds of flowers, they presented it to the father. It was proper therefore that the noble athletes, having endured a manifold strife, and conquered grandly, should receive the crown, great and incorruptible.

"Maturus, therefore, and Sanctus and Blandina and Attalus were led to the amphitheater to be exposed to the wild beasts, and to give to the heathen public a spectacle of cruelty, a day for fighting with wild beasts being specially appointed on account of our people. Both Maturus and Sanctus passed again through every torment in the amphitheater, as if they had suffered nothing before, or rather, as if, having already conquered their antagonist in many contests, they were now striving for the crown itself. They endured again the customary running of the gauntlet and the violence of the wild beasts, and everything which the furious people called for or desired, and at last, the iron chair in which their bodies being roasted, tormented them with the fumes. And not with this did the persecutors cease, but were yet more mad against them, determined to overcome their patience. But even thus they did not hear a word from Sanctus except the confession which he had uttered from the beginning. These, then, after their life had continued for a long time through the great conflict, were at last sacrificed, having been made throughout that day a spectacle to the world, in place of the usual variety of combats.

"But Blandina was suspended on a stake, and exposed to be devoured by the wild beasts that should attack her. And because she appeared as if hanging on a cross, and because of her earnest prayers, she inspired the combatants with great zeal. For they looked on her in her conflict, and beheld with their outward eyes, in the form of their sister, him who was crucified for them, that he might persuade those who believe on him, that everyone who suffers for the glory of Christ has fellowship always with the living God. As none of the wild beasts at that time touched her, she was taken down from the stake, and cast again into prison. She was preserved thus for another contest, that, being victorious in more conflicts, she might make the punishment of the crooked serpent irrevocable; and, though small and weak and despised, yet clothed with Christ the mighty and conquering Athlete, she might arouse the zeal of the brethren, and, having overcome the adversary many times might receive, through her conflict, the crown incorruptible.

"But Attalus was called for loudly by the people, because he was a person of distinction. He entered the contest readily on account of a good conscience and his genuine practice in Christian discipline, and as he had always been a witness for the truth among us. He was led around the amphitheater, a tablet being carried before him on which was written in the Roman language 'This is Attalus the Christian,' and the people were filled with indignation against him. But when the governor learned that he was a Roman, he commanded him to be taken back with the rest of those who were in prison concerning whom he had written to Caesar, and whose answer he was awaiting.

"But the intervening time was not wasted nor fruitless to them; for by their patience the measureless compassion of Christ was manifested. For through their continued life the dead were made alive, and the witnesses showed favor to those who had failed to witness. And the virgin mother had much joy in receiving alive those whom she had brought forth as dead. For through their influence many who had denied were restored, and re-begotten, and rekindled with life, and learned to confess. And being made alive and strengthened, they went to the judgment seat to be again interrogated by the governor; God, who desires not the death of the sinner, but mercifully invites to repentance, treating them with kindness. For Caesar commanded that they should be put to death, but that any who might deny should be set free. Therefore, at the beginning of the public festival which took place there, and which was attended by crowds of men from all nations, the governor brought the blessed ones to the judgment seat, to make of them a show and spectacle for the multitude. Wherefore also he examined them again, and beheaded those who appeared to possess Roman citizenship, but he sent the others to the wild beasts.

"And Christ was glorified greatly in those who had formerly denied him, for, contrary to the expectation of the heathen, they confessed. For they were examined by themselves, as about to be set free; but confessing, they were added to the order of the witnesses. But some continued without, who had never possessed a trace of faith, nor any apprehension of the wedding garment, nor an understanding of the fear of God; but, as sons of perdition, they blasphemed the Way through their apostasy. But all the others were added to the Church. While these were being examined, a certain Alexander, a Phrygian by birth, and physician by profession, who had resided in Gaul for many years, and was well known to all on account of his love to God and boldness of speech (for he was not without a share of apostolic grace), standing before the judgment seat, and by signs encouraging them to confess, appeared to those standing by as if in travail. But the people being enraged because those who formerly denied now confessed, cried out against Alexander as if he were the cause of this. Then the governor summoned him and inquired who he was. And when he answered that he was a Christian, being very angry he condemned him to the wild beasts. And on the next day he entered along with Attalus. For to please the people, the governor had ordered Attalus again to the wild beasts. And they were tortured in the amphitheater with all the instruments contrived for that purpose, and having endured a very great conflict, were at last sacrificed. Alexander neither groaned nor murmured in any manner, but communed in his heart with God. But when Attalus was placed in the iron seat, and the fumes arose from his burning body, he said to the people in the Roman language: 'Lo! This which you do is devouring men; but we do not devour men nor do any other wicked thing.' And being asked, what name God has, he replied, 'God has not a name as man has.'

"After all these, on the last day of the contests, Blandina was again brought in, with Ponticus, a boy about fifteen years old. They had been brought every day to witness the sufferings of the others, and had been pressed to swear by the idols. But because they remained steadfast and despised them, the multitude became furious, so that they had no compassion for the youth of the boy nor respect for the sex of the woman. Therefore they exposed them to all the terrible sufferings and took them through the entire round of torture, repeatedly urging them to swear, but being unable to effect this; for Ponticus, encouraged by his sister so that even the heathen could see that she was confirming and strengthening him, having nobly endured every torture, gave up the ghost. But the blessed Blandina, last of all, having, as a noble mother, encouraged her children and sent them before her victorious King, endured herself all their conflicts and hastened after them, glad and rejoicing in her departure as if called to a marriage supper, rather than cast to wild beasts. And, after the scourging, after the wild beasts, after the roasting seat, she was finally enclosed in a net, and thrown before a bull. And having been tossed about by the animal, but feeling none of the things which were happening to her, on account of her hope and firm hold upon what had been entrusted to her, and her communion with Christ, she also was sacrificed. And the heathen themselves confessed that never among them had a woman endured so many and such terrible tortures.

"But not even thus was their madness and cruelty toward the saints satisfied. For, incited by the Wild Beast, wild and barbarous tribes were not easily appeased, and their violence found another peculiar opportunity in the dead bodies. For, through their lack of manly reason, the fact that they had been conquered did not put them to shame, but rather the more enkindled their wrath as that of a wild beast, and aroused alike the hatred of governor and people to treat us unjustly; that the Scripture might be fulfilled: 'He that is lawless, let him be lawless still, and he that is righteous, let him be righteous still.' For they cast to the dogs those who had died of suffocation in the prison, carefully guarding them by night and day, lest any one should be buried by us. And they exposed the remains left by the wild beasts and by fire, mangled and charred, and placed the heads of the others by their bodies, and guarded them in like manner from burial by a watch of soldiers for many days. And some raged and gnashed their teeth against them, desiring to execute more severe vengeance upon them; but others laughed and mocked at them, magnifying their own idols, and imputed to them the punishment of the Christians. Even the more reasonable, and those who had seemed to sympathize somewhat, reproached them often, saying, 'Where is their God, and what has their religion, which they have chosen rather than life, profited them?' So various was their conduct toward us; but we were in deep affliction because we could not bury the bodies. For neither did night avail us for this purpose, nor did money persuade, nor entreaty move to compassion; but they kept watch in every way, as if the prevention of the burial would be of some advantage to them."

In addition, they say after other things: "The bodies of the martyrs, having thus in every manner been exhibited and exposed for six days, were afterward burned and reduced to ashes, and swept into the Rhone by the wicked men, so that no trace of them might appear on the earth. And this they did, as if able to conquer God, and prevent their new birth; 'that,' as they said, 'they may have no hope of a resurrection, through trust in which they bring to us this foreign and new religion, and despise terrible things, and are ready even to go to death with joy. Now let us see if they will rise again, and if their God is able to help them, and to deliver them out of our hand.'"

Questions for the Martyrs of Gaul

1. Can we imagine such horrible violence against innocent people occurring in our own day?
2. Were the deaths of these martyrs "tragedies"?
3. In light of their deaths, reflect upon what makes death "meaningful."

St. Athanasius

The great bishop of Alexandria, St. Athanasius (297–373), was a friend of the hermit St. Anthony, whose retreat to the Egyptian desert to devote his life in poverty and simplicity to prayer and service bore fruit in a flowering of holiness as the monastic life spread throughout Egypt and surrounding lands. After St. Anthony's death at the age of over one hundred years, St. Athanasius composed a short biography of his friend's life. The following excerpt describes St. Anthony's wisdom and sets forth how this wisdom, formed by a life of sacrifice, enabled him to die well.

THUS, THEREFORE, ANTHONY WARNED THE CRUEL. But the rest who came to him he so instructed that they straightway forgot their lawsuits, and felicitated those who were in retirement from the world. And he championed those who were wronged in such a way that you would imagine that he, and not the others, was the sufferer. Further, he was able to be of such use to all, that many soldiers and men who had great possessions laid aside the burdens of life, and became monks for the rest of their days. And it was as if a physician had been given by God to Egypt. For who in grief met Anthony and did not return rejoicing? Who came mourning for his dead and did not forthwith put off his

From: *Athanasius: Select Words and Letters*, Vol. 4 of *Nicene and Post-Nicene Fathers*, ed. Philip Schaff (Peabody, MA: Hendrickson, 1994), trans. H. Ellershaw, pp. 219–221.

sorrow? Who came in anger and was not converted to friendship? What poor and low-spirited man met him who, hearing him and looking upon him, did not despise wealth and console himself in his poverty? What monk, having being neglectful, came to him and became not all the stronger? What young man having come to the mountain and seen Anthony, did not forthwith deny himself pleasure and love temperance? Who when tempted by a demon, came to him and did not find rest? And who came troubled with doubts and did not get quietness of mind?

For this was the wonderful thing in Anthony's discipline, that, as I said before, having the gift of discerning spirits, he recognized their movements, and was not ignorant whither any one of them turned his energy and made his attack. And not only was he not deceived by them himself, but cheering those who were troubled with doubts, he taught them how to defeat their plans, telling them of the weakness and craft of those who possessed them. Thus each one, as though prepared by him for battle, came down from the mountain, braving the designs of the devil and his demons. How many maidens who had suitors, having but seen Anthony from afar, remained maidens for Christ's sake? And people came also from foreign parts to him, and like all others, having got some benefit, returned, as though set forward by a father. And certainly when he died, all as having been bereft of a father, consoled themselves solely by their remembrances of him, preserving at the same time his counsel and advice.

It is worthwhile that I should relate, and that you, as you wish it, should hear what his death was like. For this end of his is worthy of imitation. According to his custom he visited the monks in the outer mountain, and having learned from Providence that his own end was at hand, he said to the brethren, "This is my last visit to you which I shall make. And I shall be surprised if we see each other again in this life. At length the time of my departure is at hand, for I am near a hundred and five years old." And when they heard it they wept, and embraced, and kissed the old man. But he, as though sailing from a foreign city to his own, spoke joyously, and exhorted them "Not to grow idle in their labours, nor to become faint in their training, but to live as though dying daily. And as he had said before, zealously to guard the soul from foul thoughts, eagerly to imitate the Saints, and to have nought to do with the Meletian schismatics, for you know their wicked and profane character. Nor have any fellowship with the Arians, for their impiety is clear to all. Nor be disturbed if you see the judges protect them, for it shall cease, and their pomp is mortal and of short duration. Wherefore keep yourselves all the more untainted by them, and observe the traditions of the fathers, and chiefly the holy faith in our Lord Jesus Christ, which you have learned from the Scripture, and of which you have often been put in mind by me."

But when the brethren were urging him to abide with them and there to die, he suffered it not for many other reasons, as he showed by keeping silence, and especially for this:—The Egyptians are wont to honor with funeral rites, and to wrap in linen cloths at death the bodies of good men, and especially of the holy martyrs; and not to bury them underground, but to place them on couches, and to keep them in their houses, thinking in this to honor the departed. And Anthony often urged the bishops to give commandment to the people on this matter. In like manner he taught the laity and reproved the women, saying, "that this thing was neither lawful nor holy at all. For the bodies of the patriarchs and prophets are until now preserved in tombs, and the very body of the Lord was laid in a tomb, and a stone was laid upon it, and hid it until He rose on the third day." And thus saying, he showed that he who did not bury the bodies of the dead after death transgressed the law, even though they were sacred. For what is greater or more sacred than the body of the Lord? Many therefore having heard, henceforth buried the dead underground, and gave thanks to the Lord that they had been taught rightly.

But he, knowing the custom, and fearing that his body would be treated this way, hastened, and having bidden farewell to the monks in the outer mountain entered the inner mountain, where he was accustomed to abide. And after a few months he fell sick. Having summoned those who were there—they were two in number who had remained in the mountain fifteen years, practicing the discipline and attending on Anthony on account of his age—he said to them, "I, as it is written, go the way of the fathers, for I perceive that I am called by the Lord. And do you be watchful and destroy not your long discipline, but as though now making a beginning, zealously preserve your determination. For you know the treachery of the demons, how fierce they are, but how little power they have. Wherefore fear them not, but rather ever breathe Christ, and trust Him. Live as though dying daily. Give heed to yourselves, and remember the admonition you have heard from me. Have no fellowship with the schismatics, nor any dealings at all with the heretical Arians. For you know how I shunned them on account of their hostility to Christ, and the strange doctrines of their heresy. Therefore be the more earnest always to be followers first of God and then of the Saints; that after death they also may receive you as well-known friends into the eternal habitations. Ponder over these things and think of them, and if you have any care for me and are mindful of me as of a father, suffer no one to take my body into Egypt, lest they place me in the houses, for to avoid this I entered into the mountain and came here. Moreover you know how I always put to rebuke those who had this custom, and exhorted them to cease from it. Bury my body, therefore, and hide it underground yourselves, and let my words be observed by you that no one may know the place but you alone. For at the resurrection of the dead I shall receive it incorruptible from the Saviour. And divide my garments. To Athanasius the bishop give one sheepskin and the garment whereon I am laid, which he himself gave me new, but which with me has grown old. To Serapion the bishop give the other sheepskin, and keep the hair garment yourselves. For the rest fare you well, my children, for Anthony is departing, and is with you no more."

Having said this, when they had kissed him, he lifted up his feet, and as though he saw friends coming to him and was glad because of them—for as he lay his countenance appeared joyful—he died and was gathered to the fathers. And they afterward, according to his commandment, wrapped him up and buried him hiding his body underground. And no one knows to this day where it was buried, save those two only. But each of those who received the sheepskin of the blessed Anthony and the garment worn by him guards it as a precious treasure. For even to look on them is as it were to behold Anthony; and he who is clothed in them seems with joy to bear his admonitions.

This is the end of Anthony's life in the body and the above was the beginning of the discipline. Even if this account is small compared with his merit, still from this reflect how great Anthony, the man of God, was. Who from his youth to so great an age preserved a uniform zeal for the discipline, and neither through old age was subdued by the desire of costly food, nor through the infirmity of his body changed the fashion of his clothing, nor washed even his feet with water, and yet remained entirely free from harm. For his eyes were undimmed and quite sound and he saw clearly; of his teeth he had not lost one, but they had become worn to the gums through the great age of the old man. He remained strong both in hands and feet; and while all men were using various foods, and washings and divers garments, he appeared more cheerful and of greater strength. And the fact that his fame has been blazoned everywhere; that all regard him with wonder, and that those who have never seen him long for him, is clear proof of his virtue and God's love of his soul. For not from writings, nor from worldly wisdom, nor through any art, was Anthony renowned, but solely from his piety towards God. That this was the gift of God no one will deny. For from whence into Spain and into Gaul, how into Rome and Africa, was the man heard of who abode hidden in a mountain, unless it was God who makes His own known everywhere, who also promised this to Anthony at the beginning? For even if they work secretly, even if they wish to remain in obscurity, yet the Lord shows them as lamps to lighten all, that those who hear may thus know that the precepts of God are able to make men prosper and thus be zealous in the pate of virtue.

Read these words, therefore, to the rest of the brethren that they may learn what the life of monks ought to be; and may believe that our Lord and Savior Jesus Christ glorifies those who glorify Him, and leads those who serve Him unto the end, not only to the kingdom of heaven, but here also—even though they hide themselves and are desirous of withdrawing from the world—makes them illustrious and well known everywhere on account of their virtue and the help they render others. And if need be, read this among the heathen, that even in this way they may learn that our Lord Jesus Christ is not only God and the Son of God, but also that the Christians who truly serve Him and religiously believe on Him, prove, not only that the demons, whom the Greeks themselves think to be gods, are no gods, but also tread them under foot and put them to flight as deceivers and corrupters of mankind, through Jesus Christ our Lord, to whom be glory for ever and ever. Amen.

Questions for St. Athanasius

1. At the beginning of this excerpt, how does the author describe St. Anthony's justice or holiness?
2. How is this justice or holiness manifested in St. Anthony's dying?
3. What is the source of St. Anthony's justice, that sustains him in his dying?

St. Ambrose

Bishop of Milan and a magnificent theologian, St. Ambrose (340–397) is best known perhaps for having instructed and baptized St. Augustine. In the culture of the time, influenced by Stoic philosophy, mourning for the dead was sometimes discouraged. Preaching this eulogy for his beloved brother, St. Ambrose exhibits the intense mourning proper to a Christian. His sadness reminds him that the entire Church on earth grieves the loss of his brother—when one member suffers, all suffer—and yet God is gathering together the Church in Heaven. Through our mourning for the death of others, we learn to desire our heavenly homecoming.

WE HAVE BROUGHT HITHER, dearest brethren, my sacrifice, a sacrifice undefiled, a sacrifice well pleasing to God, my lord and brother Satyrus. I did not forget that he was mortal, nor did my feelings deceive me, but grace abounded more exceedingly. And so I have nothing to complain of, but have cause for thankfulness to God, for I always desired that if any troubles should await either the Church or myself, they should rather fall on me and on my house. Thanks, therefore, be to God, that in this time of common fear, when everything is dreaded from the

From: *The Two Books of St. Ambrose, Bishop of Milan, on the Decease of His Brother Satyrus*, Book 1, in *Nicene and Post-Nicene Fathers*, Second Series, Vol. 1: *Ambrose: Select Works and Letters*, eds. Philip Schaff and Henry Wace (Peabody, MA: Hendrickson, 1995 [1896]): pp. 161–162, 171–173.

barbarian movements, I ended the trouble of all by my personal grief, and that I dreaded for all which was turned upon me. And may this be fully accomplished, so that my grief may be a ransom for the grief of all.

Nothing among things of earth, dearest brethren, was more precious to me, nothing more worthy of love, nothing more dear than such a brother, but public matters come before private. And should any one enquire what was his feeling; he would rather be slain for others than live for himself, because Christ died according to the flesh for all, that we might learn not to live for ourselves alone.

To this must be added that I cannot be ungrateful to God; for I must rather rejoice that I had such a brother than grieve that I had lost a brother, for the former is a gift, the latter a debt to be paid. And so, as long as I might, I enjoyed the loan entrusted to me, now He Who deposited the pledge has taken it back. There is no difference between denying that a pledge has been deposited and grieving at its being returned. In each there is untrustworthiness, and in each [eternal] life is risked. It is a fault if you refuse repayment, and piety if you refuse a sacrifice. Since, too, the lender of money can be made a fool of, but the Author of nature, the Lender of all that we need, cannot be cheated. And so the larger the amount of the loan, so much the more gratitude is due for the use of the capital.

Wherefore, I cannot be ungrateful concerning my brother, for he has given back that which was common to nature, and has gained what is peculiar to grace alone. For who would refuse that common lot? Who would grieve that a pledge specially entrusted to him is taken away, since the Father gave up His only Son to death for us? Who would think he ought to be excepted from the lot of dying, who has not been excepted from the lot of being born? It is a great mystery of divine love, that not even in Christ was exception made of the death of the body; and although He was the Lord of nature, He refused not the law of the flesh which He had taken upon Him. It is necessary for me to die, for Him it was not necessary. Could not He Who said of His servant, "If I will that he tarry thus until I come, what is it to you?" not have remained as He was, if so He willed? But by continuance of my brother's life here, he would have destroyed his reward and my sacrifice. What is a greater consolation to us than that according to the flesh Christ also died? Or why should I weep too violently for my brother, knowing as I do that that divine love could not die.

Why should I alone weep more than others for him for whom you all weep? I have merged my personal grief in the grief of all, especially because my tears are of no use, whereas yours strengthen faith and bring consolation. You who are rich weep, and by weeping prove that riches gathered together are of no avail for safety, since death cannot be put off by a money payment, and the last day carries off alike the rich and the poor. You that are old weep, because in him you fear that you see the lot of your own children; and for this reason, since you cannot prolong the life of the body, train your children not to bodily enjoyment but to virtuous duties. And you that are young weep too, because the end of life is not the ripeness of old age. The poor too wept, and, which is of much more worth, and much more fruitful, washed away his transgressions with their tears. Those are redeeming tears, those are groanings which hide the grief of death, that grief which through the plenteousness of eternal joy covers over the feeling of former grief. And so, though the funeral be that of a private person, yet is the mourning public; and therefore cannot the weeping last long which is hallowed by the affection of all.

For why should I weep for you, my most loving brother, who was thus torn from me that you might be the brother of all? For I have not lost but changed my intercourse with you; before we were inseparable in the body, now we are undivided in affection; for you remain with me, and ever will remain. And, indeed, while you were living with me, our country never tore you from me, nor did you yourself ever prefer our country to me; and now you are become surety for that other country, for I begin to be no stranger there where the better portion of myself already is. I was never wholly engrossed in myself, but the greater part of each of us was in the other, yet we were each of us in Christ, in Whom is the whole sum of all, and the portion of each severally. This grave is more pleasing to me than your natal soil, in which is the fruit not of nature but of grace, for in that body which now lies lifeless lies the better work of my life, since in this body, too, which I bear is the richer portion of yourself.

And would that, as memory and gratitude are devoted to you, so, too, whatever time I have still to breathe this air, I could breathe it into your life, and that half of my time might be struck off from me and added to yours! For it had been just that for those, whose use of hereditary property was always undivided, the period of life should not have been divided, or at least that we, who always without difference shared everything in common during life, should not have a difference in our deaths.

But now, brother, whither shall I advance, or whither shall I turn? The ox seeks his fellow, and conceives itself incomplete, and by frequent lowing shows its tender longing, if perchance that one is wanting with whom it has been wont to draw the plough. And shall I, my brother, not long after you? Or can I ever forget you, with whom I always drew the plough of this life? In work I was inferior, but in love more closely bound; not so much fit through my strength, as endurable through your patience, who with the care of anxious affection did ever protect my side with yours, as a father in your care, as older in watchfulness, as younger in respect. So in the one degree of relationship you did expend on me the duties of many, so that I long after not one only but many lost in you, in whom alone flattery was unknown, dutifulness was portrayed. For you had nothing to which to add by pretence, inasmuch as all was comprised in your dutifulness, so as neither to receive addition nor await a change.

But whither am I going, in my immoderate grief, forgetful of my duty, mindful of kindness received? The Apostle calls me back, and as it were puts a bit upon my sorrow, saying, as you heard just now: "We would not that you should be ignorant, brethren, concerning them that sleep, that you be not sorrowful, as the rest which have no hope" (1 Thess 4:14). Pardon me, dearest brethren. For we are not all able to say: "Be you imitators of me, as I also am of Christ" (1 Cor 4:16). But if you seek to imitate, you have One whom you may imitate. All are not fitted to teach, would that all were apt to learn.

But we have not incurred any grievous sin by our tears. Not all weeping proceeds from unbelief or weakness. Natural grief is one thing, distrustful sadness is another, and there is a very great difference between longing for what you have lost and lamenting that you have lost it. Not only grief has tears, joy also has tears of its own. Both piety excites weeping, and prayer waters the couch, and supplication, according to the prophet's saying, washes the bed (Ps 6:6). Their friends made a great mourning when the patriarchs were buried. Tears, then, are marks of devotion, not producers of grief. I confess, then, that I too wept, but the Lord also wept. He wept for one not related to Him, I for my brother. He wept for all in weeping for one, I weep for you in all, my brother.

For one, then, who has performed such good deeds, and is rescued from perils, I shall weep rather from longing for him than for the loss.

For the very opportuneness of his death bids us bear in mind that we must follow him rather with grateful veneration than grieve for him, for it is written that private grief should cease in public sorrow. This is said in the prophetical language, not only to that one woman, who is figured there, but to each, since it seems to be said to the Church.

To me, then, does this message come, and Holy Scripture says: "Do you teach this, is it thus that you instruct the people of God? Do you not know that your example is a danger to others? Save that perhaps you complain that your prayer is not heard. First of all this is shameless arrogance, to desire to obtain for yourself what you know to have been denied to many, even saints, when you are aware that God is no respecter of persons?" For although God is merciful, yet if He always heard all, He would appear to act no longer of His own free will, but by a kind of necessity. Then, since all ask, if He were to hear all, no one would die. For how much do you daily pray? Is, then, God's appointment to be made void in consideration of you? Why, then, do you lament that that is sometimes not obtained, which you know cannot always be obtained?

"You fool," it says, "above all women, do you not see our mourning, and what has happened to us, how that Sion our mother is saddened with all sadness, and humbled with humbling. Mourn now also very sore, since we all mourn, and be sad since we all are sad, and you are grieved for a brother. Ask the earth and she shall tell you that it is she which ought to mourn, outliving so many that grow upon her. And out of her," it says, "were all born in the beginning, and out of her shall others come, and, behold, they walk almost all into destruction, and a multitude of them is utterly rooted out. Who, then, ought to make more mourning than she that has lost so great a multitude, and not you, who are sorry but for one?"[1]

Let, then, the common mourning swallow up ours and cut off the bitterness of our private sorrow. For we ought not to grieve for those whom we see to be set free, and we bear in mind that so many holy souls are not without a purpose at this time loosed from the chains of the body. For we see, as if by God's decree, such reverend widows dying so closely at one time, that it seems to be a sort of setting out on a journey, not a sinking in death, lest their chastity in which they have served God their full time should be exposed to peril. What groans, what mourning, does so bitter a recollection stir up in me! And if I had not leisure for mourning, yet in my own personal grief, in the loss of the very flower of so much merit, the common lot of nature consoled me; and my grief in consideration of one alone veiled the bitterness of the public funeral by the show of piety at home.

I seek again, then, O sacred Scripture, your consolations, for it delights me to dwell on your precepts and your sentences. How far more easy is it for heaven and earth to pass away, than for one tittle of the law to fail! But let us now listen to what is written: "Now," it says, "keep your sorrow to yourself, and bear with a good courage the things which have befallen you. For if you shall acknowledge the determination of God to be just, you shall both receive your son in time, and shall be praised among women."[2] If this is said to a woman, how much more to a priest! If such words are said of a son it is certainly not unfitting that they should be uttered also concerning the loss of a brother; though if he had been my son I could never have loved him more. For as in the death of children, the lost labour and the pain borne to no purpose seem to increase the sorrow; so, too, in the case of brothers the habits of intercourse and joint occupations inflame the bitterness of grief.

But, lo! I hear the Scripture saying: "Do not continue this discourse, but allow yourself to be persuaded. For how great are the misfortunes of Sion! Be comforted in regard of the sorrow of Jerusalem. For you see that our holy places are polluted and the name that was called upon us is almost profaned, they that are ours have suffered shame, our priests are burnt, our Levites gone into captivity, our wives are polluted, our virgins suffer violence, our righteous men are carried away, our little ones given up, our young men become weak. And, which is the greatest of all, the seal of Sion has lost her glory, since now she is delivered into the hands of them that hate us. Do you, then, shake off your great heaviness, and put from you the multitude of sorrows, that the Mighty may be merciful to you again, and the Highest shall give you rest by easing your labours."[3]

So, then, my tears shall cease, for one must yield to healthful remedies, since there ought to be some difference between believers and unbelievers. Let them, therefore, weep who cannot have the hope of the resurrection, of which not the sentence of God but the strictness of the faith deprives them. Let there be this difference between the servants of Christ and the worshippers of idols, that the latter weep for their friends, whom they suppose to have perished forever; that they should never cease from tears, and gain no rest from sorrow, who think that the dead have no rest. But from us, for whom death is the end not of our nature but of this life only, since our nature itself is restored to a better state, let the advent of death wipe away all tears.

And certainly if they have ever found any consolation who have thought that death is the end of sensation and the failing of our nature, how much more must we find it so to whom the consciousness of good done brings the promise of better rewards! The heathen have their consolation, because they think that death is a cessation of all evils, and as they are without the fruit of life, so, too, they think that they have escaped all the feeling and pain of those severe and constant sufferings which we have to endure in this life. We, however, as we are better supported by our rewards, so, too, ought we to be more patient through our consolation, for they seem to be not lost but sent before, who death is not going to swallow up, but eternity to receive.

My tears shall therefore cease, or if they cannot cease, I will weep for you, my brother, in the common sorrow, and will hide my private groaning in the public good. For how can my tears wholly cease, since they break forth at every utterance of your name, or when my very habitual actions arouse your memory, or when my affection pictures your likeness, or when recollection renews my grief? For how can you be absent who are again made present in so many occupations? You are present, I say, and are always brought before me, and with my whole mind and soul do I embrace you, gaze upon you, address you, kiss you; I grasp you whether in the gloomy night or in the clear light, when you vouchsafe to revisit and console me sorrowing. And now the very nights which used to seem irksome in your lifetime, because they denied us the power of looking on each other; and sleep itself, lately, the odious interrupter of our converse, have commenced to be sweet, because they restore you to me. They, then, are not wretched but blessed whose mutual presence fails not, whose care for each other is not lessened, whose mutual esteem is increased. For sleep is like a likeness and image of death.

But if, in the quiet of night, our souls still cleaving to the chains of the body, and as it were bound within the prison bars of the limbs, yet are able to see higher and separate things, how much more do they see these, when in their pure and heavenly senses they suffer from no hindrances of bodily weakness. And so when, as a certain evening was drawing on, I was complaining that you did not revisit me when at rest, you were wholly present always. So that, as I lay with my limbs bathed in sleep, while I was in mind awake for you, you were alive to me, I could say, "What is death, my brother?" For certainly you were not separated from me for a single moment, for you were so present with me everywhere, that that enjoyment of each other, which we were unable to have in the intercourse of this life, is now always and everywhere with us. For at that time certainly all things could not be present, for neither did our physical constitution allow it, nor could the sight of each other, nor the sweetness of our bodily embraces at all times and in all places be enjoyed. But the pictures in our souls were always present with us, even when we were not together, and these have not come to an end, but constantly come back to us, and the greater the longing the greater abundance have we of them.

So, then, I hold you, my brother, and neither death nor time shall tear you from me. Tears themselves are sweet, and weeping itself a pleasure, for by these the eagerness of the soul is assuaged, and affection being eased is quieted. For neither can I be without you, nor ever forget you, or think of you without tears. O bitter days, which show that our union is broken! O nights worthy of tears, which have lost for me so good a sharer of my rest, so inseparable a companion! What sufferings would you cause me, unless the likeness of him present offered itself to me, unless the visions of my soul represented him whom my bodily sight shows me no more!

Now, now, O brother, dearest to my soul, although you are gone by too early a death, happy at least are you, who does not endure these sorrows, and are not compelled to mourn the loss of a brother, separation from whom you could not long endure, but did quickly return and visit him again. But if then you hastened to banish the weariness of my loneliness, to lighten the sadness of your brother's mind, how much more often ought you now to revisit my afflicted soul, and yourself lighten the sorrow which has its origin from you!

But the exercise of my office now bids me rest awhile, and attention to my priestly duties draws my mind away; but what will happen to my holy sister, who though she moderates her affection by the fear of God, yet again kindles the grief itself of the affection by the zeal of her devotion? Prostrate on the ground, embracing her brother's tomb, wearied with toilsome walking, sad in spirit, day and night she renews her grief. For though she often breaks off her weeping by speech, she renews it in prayer; and although in her knowledge of her Scriptures she excels those who bring consolation, she makes up for her desire of weeping by the constancy of her prayers, renewing the abundance of her tears then chiefly, when no one can interrupt her. So you have that which you may pity, not what you may blame, for to weep in prayer is a sign of virtue. And although that be a common thing with virgins, whose softer sex and more tender affection abound in tears at the sight of the common weakness, even without the feeling of family grief, yet when there is a greater cause for sorrowing, no limit is set to that sorrow.

The means of consolation, then, are wanting since excuses abound. For you cannot forbid that which you teach, especially when she attributes her tears to devotion, not to sorrow, and conceals the course of the common grief for fear of shame. Console her, therefore, you who can approach her soul, and penetrate her mind. Let her perceive that you are present, feel that you are not departed, that having enjoyed his consolation of whose merit she is assured, she may learn not to grieve heavily for him, who warned her that he was not to be mourned for.

But why should I delay you, brother, why should I wait that my address should die and as it were be buried with you? Although the sight and form of your lifeless body, and its remaining comeliness and figure abiding here, comfort the eyes, I delay no longer, let us go on to the tomb. But first, before the people I utter the last farewell, declare peace to you, and pay the last kiss. God before us to that home, common and waiting for all, and certainly now longed for by me beyond others. Prepare a common dwelling for him with whom you have dwelt, and as here we have had all things in common, so there, too, let us know no divided rights.

Do not, I pray you, long put off him who is desirous of you, expect him who is hastening after you, help him who is hurrying, and if I seem to you to delay too long, summon me. For we have not ever been long separated from each other, but you were always wont to return. Nor since you cannot return again, I will go to you; it is just that I should repay the kindness and take my turn. Never was there much difference in the condition of our life; whether health or sickness, it was common to both, so that if one sickened the other fell ill, and when one began to recover, the other, too, was convalescent. How have we lost our rights? This time, too, we had our sickness in common, how is it that death was not ours in common?

And now to You, Almighty God, I commend this guileless soul, to You I offer my sacrifice; accept favourably and mercifully the gift of a brother, the offering of a priest. I offer beforehand these first libations of myself. I come to You with this pledge, a pledge not of money but of life, cause me not to remain too long a debtor of such an amount. It is not the ordinary interest of a brother's love, nor the common course of nature, which is increased by such an amount of virtue. I can bear it, if I shall be soon compelled to pay it.

Questions for St. Ambrose

1. How does Ambrose oscillate between grieving and consolation?
2. What is Ambrose's consolation? How does Ambrose's mourning lead him to desire union with God more intensely?
3. What is the purpose of a eulogy?

Notes

1. 2 Esdras 10:6–11.
2. 2 Esdras 10:15, 16.
3. 2 Esdras 10:20–24.

St. Augustine

St. Augustine, the greatest theologian of the early Church and bishop of the North Africa city of Hippo, here describes the death of his mother at age 56 and his mourning. In her dying, St. Monica reveals that her Christian life had not been spent in vain; she has learned to desire God. St. Augustine's response to his beloved mother's death is a whirlwind of emotion. He tries to recall that she is alive in God, but he is swept away nonetheless by powerful torrents of grief and loss. He discovers in the end that such grief belongs to the process by which we lay bare our hearts before God and are strengthened to cleave to what truly matters in life.

AT THE END WHEN HER HUSBAND HAD REACHED the end of his life in time, she succeeded in gaining him for you. After he was a baptized believer, she had no cause to complain of behavior which she had tolerated in one not yet a believer. She was also a servant of your servants: any of them who knew her found much to praise in her, held her in honor and loved her; for they felt your presence in her heart, witnessed by the fruits of her holy way of life. She had been "the wife of one husband" (1 Tim. 5:9). She repaid the mutual debt to her parents; she had governed her house in a spirit of devotion (1 Tim. 5:4). She

Excerpts from Saint Augustine, *Confessions*, trans. Henry Chadwick (Oxford: Oxford University Press, 1998), pp. 170–178. Used with permission of Oxford University Press.

had "testimony to her good works" (1 Tim. 5:10). She had brought up her children, enduring travail as often as she saw them wandering away from you. Lastly, Lord—by your gift you allow me to speak for your servants, for before her falling asleep we were bound together in community in you after receiving the grace of baptism—she exercised care for everybody as if they were all her own children. She served us as if she was a daughter to all of us.

The day was imminent when she was to depart this life (the day which you knew and we did not). It came about, as I believe by your providence through your hidden ways, that she and I were standing leaning out of a window overlooking a garden. It was at the house where we were staying at Ostia on the Tiber, where, far removed from the crowds, after the exhaustion of a long journey, we were recovering our strength for the voyage.

Alone with each other, we talked very intimately. "Forgetting the past and reaching forward to what lies ahead" (Phil. 3:13), we were searching together in the presence of the truth which is you yourself. We asked what quality of life the eternal life of the saints will have, a life which "neither eye has seen nor ear heard, not has it entered into the heart of man" (1 Cor. 2:9). But with the mouth of the heart wide open, we drank in the waters flowing from your spring on high, "the spring of life" (Ps. 35:10) which is with you. Sprinkled with this dew to the limit of our capacity, our minds attempted in some degree to reflect on so great a reality.

The conversation led us towards the conclusion that the pleasure of the bodily senses, however delightful in the radiant light of this physical world, is seen by comparison with the life of eternity to be not even worth considering. Our minds were lifted up by an ardent affection towards eternal being itself. Step by step we climbed beyond all corporeal objects and the heaven itself, where sun, moon, and stars shed light on the earth. We ascended even further by internal reflection and dialogue and wonder at your works, and we entered into our own minds. We moved up beyond them so as to attain to the region of inexhaustible abundance where you feed Israel eternally with truth for food. There life is the wisdom by which all creatures come into being, both things which were and which will be. But wisdom itself is not brought into being but is as it was and always will be. Furthermore, in this wisdom there is no past and future, but only being, since it is eternal. For to exist in the past or in the future is no property of the eternal. And while we talked and panted after it, we touched it in some small degree by a moment of total concentration of the heart. And we sighed and left behind us "the first-fruits of the Spirit" (Rom. 8:23) bound to that higher world, as we returned to the noise of our human speech where a sentence has both a beginning and an ending. But what is to be compared with your word, Lord of our lives? It dwells in you without growing old and gives renewal to all things.

Therefore we said: If to anyone the tumult of the flesh has fallen silent, if the images of earth, water, and air are quiescent, if the heavens themselves are shut out and the very soul itself is making no sound and is surpassing itself by no longer thinking about itself, if all dreams and visions in the imagination are excluded, if all language and every sign and everything transitory is silent—for if anyone could hear them, this is what all of them would be saying, "We did not make ourselves, we were made by him who abides for eternity" (Ps. 79:3, 5)—if after this declaration they were to keep silence, having directed our ears to him that made them, then he alone would speak not through them but through himself. We would hear his word, not through the tongue of the flesh, nor through the voice of an angel, nor through the sound of thunder, not through the obscurity of a symbolic utterance. Him who in these things we love we would hear in person without their mediation. That is how it was when at that moment we extended our reach and in a flash of mental energy attained the eternal wisdom which abides beyond all things. If only it could last, and other visions of a vastly inferior kind could be withdrawn! Then this alone could ravish and absorb and enfold in inward joys the person granted the vision. So too eternal life is of the quality of that moment of understanding after which we sighed. Is not this the meaning of "Enter into the joy of your Lord" (Matt. 25:21)? And when is that to be? Surely it is when "we all rise again, but are not all changed" (1 Cor. 15:51).

I said something like this, even if not in just this way and with exactly these words. Yet, Lord, you know that on that day when we had this conversation, and this world with all its delights became worthless to us as we talked on, my mother said "My son, as for myself, I now find no pleasure in this life. What I have still to do here and why I am here, I do not know. My hope in this world is already fulfilled. The one reason why I wanted to stay longer in this life was my desire to see you a Catholic

Christian before I die. My God has granted this in a way more than I had hoped. For I see you despising this world's success to become his servant. What have I to do here?"

The reply I made to that I do not well recall, for within five days or not much more she fell sick of a fever. While she was ill, on one day she suffered loss of consciousness and gradually became unaware of things around her. We ran to be with her, but she quickly recovered consciousness. She looked at me and my brother standing beside her, and said to us in the manner of someone looking for something, "Where was I?" Then seeing us struck dumb with grief, she said: "Bury your mother here." I kept silence and fought back my tears. But my brother, as if to cheer her up, said something to the effect that he hoped she would be buried not in a foreign land but in her home country. When she heard that, her face became worried and her eyes looked at him in reproach that he should think that. She looked in my direction and said "See what he says," and soon said to both of us "Bury my body anywhere you like. Let no anxiety about that disturb you. I have only one request to make of you, that you remember me at the altar of the Lord, wherever you may be." She explained her thought in such words as she could speak, then fell silent as the pain of her sickness became worse.

But as I thought about your gifts, invisible God, which you send into the hearts of your faithful, and which in consequence produce wonderful fruits, I was filled with joy and gave thanks to you as I recalled what I knew of the great concern which had agitated her about the tomb which she had foreseen and prepared for herself next to the body of her husband. Because they had lived together in great concord, she had expressed the wish (so little is the human mind capable of grasping divine things) that a further addition might be made to her happiness and that posterity might remember it: she wished it to be granted to her that after her travels overseas the two partners in the marriage might be joined in the same covering of earth. But when, by your bountiful goodness, this vain thought began to disappear from her mind, I did not know. I was delighted and surprised that my mother had disclosed this to me. Yet even at the time of our conversation at the window, when she said "What have I to do here now?," she made it evident that she did not want to die at home. Moreover, I later learnt that before, when we were at Ostia, she conversed one day with some of my friends with all a mother's confidence, and spoke of her contempt for this life and of the beneficence of death. I had not been present on this occasion. But they were surprised at the courage of the woman (for you had given it to her), and asked whether she were not afraid to leave her body so far from her own town. "Nothing," she said, "is distant from God, and there is no ground for fear that he may not acknowledge me at the end of the world and raise me up."

On the ninth day of her illness, when she was aged 56, and I was 33, this religious and devout soul was released from the body.

I closed her eyes and an overwhelming grief welled into my heart and was about to flow forth in floods of tears. But at the same time under a powerful act of mental control my eyes held back the flood and dried it up. The inward struggle put me into great agony. Then when she breathed her last, the boy Adeodatus cried out in sorrow and was pressed by all of us to be silent. In this way too something of the child in me, which had slipped towards weeping, was checked and silenced by the youthful voice, the voice of my heart. We did not think it right to celebrate the funeral with tearful dirges and lamentations, since in most cases it is customary to use such mourning to imply sorrow for the miserable state of those who die, or even their complete extinction. But my mother's dying meant neither that her state was miserable nor that she was suffering extinction. We were confident of this because of the evidence of her virtuous life, her "faith unfeigned" (1 Tim. 1:15), and reasons of which we felt certain.

Why then did I suffer sharp pains of inward grief? It must have been the fresh wound caused by the break in the habit formed by our living together, a very affectionate and precious bond suddenly torn apart. I was glad indeed to have her testimony when in that last sickness she lovingly responded to my attentions by calling me a devoted son. With much feeling in her love, she recalled that she had never heard me speak a harsh or bitter word to her. And yet, my God our maker, what comparison can there be between the respect with which I deferred to her and the service she rendered to me? Now that I had lost the immense support she gave, my soul was wounded, and my life as it were torn to pieces, since my life and hers had become a single thing.

After the boy's tears had been checked, Evodius took up the psalter and began to chant a psalm. The entire household responded to him: "I sing of your mercy and judgment, Lord" (Ps. 100:1).

When the news of what had happened got about, many brothers and religious women gathered and, according to custom, those whose duty it was made arrangements for the funeral. I myself went apart to a place where I could go without discourtesy and, with those who thought I ought not to be left alone, I discussed subjects fitting for the occasion. I was using truth as a fomentation to alleviate the pain of which you were aware, but of which they were not. They listened to me intently and supposed me to have no feeling of grief.

But in your ears where none of them heard me, I was reproaching the softness of my feelings and was holding back the torrent of sadness. It yielded a little to my efforts, but then again its attack swept over me—yet not so as to lead me to burst into tears or even to change the expression on my face. But I knew what pressure lay upon my heart. And because it caused me such sharp displeasure to see how much power these human frailties had over me, though they are a necessary part of the order we have to endure and are the lot of the human condition, there was another pain to put on top of my grief, and I was tortured by a twofold sadness.

When her body was carried out, we went and returned without a tear. Even during those prayers which we poured out to you when the sacrifice of our redemption was offered for her, when her corpse was placed beside the tomb prior to burial, as was the custom there, not even at those prayers did I weep. But throughout the day I was inwardly oppressed with sadness and with a troubled mind I asked you, to the utmost of my strength, to heal my pain. You did not do so. I believe that you gave me no relief so that by this single admonition I should be made aware of the truth that every habit is a fetter adverse even to the mind that is not fed upon deceit. I decided to go and take a bath, because I had heard that baths, for which the Greeks say *balaneion*, get their name from throwing anxiety out of the mind. But I confess this to your mercy, father of orphans (Ps. 67:6) that after I bathed I was exactly the same as before. The bitterness of sorrow had not sweated out of my heart. Finally, I fell asleep and on waking up found that in large part my suffering had been relieved. Alone upon my bed I remembered the very true verses of your Ambrose. For you are

> Creator of all things.
> You rule the heavens.
> You clothe the day with light
> And night with the grace of sleep.

> So rest restores exhausted limbs
> to the usefulness of work.
> It lightens weary minds
> And dissolves the causes of grief.

From then on, little by little, I was brought back to my old feelings about your handmaid, recalling her devout attitude to you and her holy gentle and considerate treatment of us, of which I had suddenly been deprived. I was glad to weep before you about her and for her, about myself and for myself. Now I let flow the tears which I had held back so that they ran as freely as they wished. My heart rested upon them, and it reclined upon them because it was your ears that were there, not those of some human critic who would put a proud interpretation on my weeping. And now, Lord, I make my confession to you in writing. Let anyone who wishes read and interpret as he pleases. If he finds fault that I wept for my mother for a fraction of an hour, the mother who had died before my eyes who had wept for me that I might live before your eyes, let him not mock me but rather, if a person of much charity, let him weep himself before you for my sins; for you are the Father of all the brothers of your Christ.

My heart is healed of that wound; I could be reproached for yielding to that emotion of physical kinship. But now, on behalf of your maidservant, I pour out to you, our God, another kind of tears. They flow from a spirit struck hard by considering the perils threatening every soul that "dies in Adam" (1 Cor. 15:22). She, being "made alive in Christ," though not yet delivered from the flesh, so lived that your name is praised in her faith and behavior. But I do not dare to say that, since the day when you regenerated her through baptism, no word came from her mouth contrary to your precept. It was said by the truth, your Son: "If anyone says to his brother, Fool, he will be liable to the gehenna of fire" (Matt. 5:22). Woe even to those of praiseworthy life if you put their life under scrutiny and remove mercy. But because you do not search our faults with rigor, we confidently hope for some place with you. If anyone lists his true merits to you, what is he enumerating before you but your gifts? If only human beings would acknowledge themselves to be but human, and that "he who glories would glory in the Lord" (2 Cor. 10:17)!

Therefore, God of my heart, my praise and my life, I set aside for a moment her good actions for which I rejoice and give you thanks. I now petition you for my mother's sins. "Hear me" (Ps 142:1) through the remedy for our wounds who hung upon the wood and sits at your right hand to intercede for us (Rom 8:34). I know that she acted mercifully and from her heart forgave the debts of her debtors (Matt. 6:12; 18:35). Now please forgive her her debts if she contracted any during the many years that passed after she received the water of salvation. Forgive, Lord, forgive, I beseech you. "Enter not into judgment" with her (Ps. 142:2). Let mercy triumph over justice (Jas. 2:13), for your words are true, and you have promised mercy to the merciful (Matt. 5:7). That the merciful should be so was your gift to them: "You have mercy on whom you will have mercy and show pity to whom you are compassionate" (Rom. 9:15; Exod. 33:19).

I believe you have already done what I am asking of you; but "approve the desires of my mouth, Lord" (Ps 118:108). As the day of her deliverance approached, she did not think of having her body sumptuously wrapped or embalmed with perfumes or given a choice monument. Nor did she care if she had a tomb in her homeland. On that she gave us no instruction; she desired only that she might be remembered at your altar which she had attended every day without fail, where she knew that what is distributed is the holy victim who "abolished the account of debts which was reckoned against us" (Col. 2:14). He triumphed over the enemy who counts up our sins, and searches for grounds of accusation, but who found no fault in him in whom we are conquerors (John 14:30; Rom. 8:37).

Who will restore to him his innocent blood? Who will restore to him the price which he paid to buy us, so as to take us out of our adversary's hands? By the chain of faith your handmaid bound her soul to the sacrament of our redemption. Let no one tear her from your protection. Let not the lion and dragon (Ps. 90:13) intrude themselves either by force or by subtle tricks. For she will not reply that she has no debts to pay, lest she be refuted and captured by the clever Accuser. Her answer will be that her debts have been forgiven by him to whom no one can repay the price which he, who owed nothing, paid on our behalf.

With her husband may she rest in peace. She had no one as her husband before him and after him. She served him by offering you "fruit with patience" (Luke 8:15) so as to gain him for you also. My Lord, my God, inspire your servants, my brothers, your sons, my masters, to whose service I dedicate my heart, voice, and writings, that all who read this book may remember at your altar Monica your servant and Patrick her late husband, through whose physical bond you brought me into this life without my knowing how. May they remember with devout affection my parents in this transient light, my kith and kin under you, our Father, in our mother the Catholic Church, and my fellow citizens in the eternal Jerusalem. For this city your pilgrim people yearn, from their leaving it to their return. So as a result of these confessions of mine may my mother's request receive a richer response through the prayers which many offer and not only those which come from me (2 Cor. 1:11).

Questions for St. Augustine

1. Reflect upon Augustine's last conversation with Monica at Ostia.
2. Describe Augustine's process of mourning.
3. Describe Augustine's prayers for his dead parents.

St. Thomas Aquinas

In his relatively short life (1225–1274), St. Thomas Aquinas composed a rich abundance of theological writings, in which he explores almost every aspect of the Christian life. Known as the "Angelic Doctor" for his serenely contemplative approach, St. Thomas's writings are known for reaching the heart of the matter with succinct clarity. His writings are marvelously dialogic: before stating his view he considers as "objections" the most prominent and persuasive opposing views. His analysis of martyrdom thus remains relevant today in light of Islamic views of martyrdom and of the continuing persecution of Christians around the world.

Article 1: Whether martyrdom is an act of virtue?

Objection 1. It seems that martyrdom is not an act of virtue. For all acts of virtue are voluntary. But martyrdom is sometimes not voluntary, as in the case of the Innocents who were slain for Christ's sake, and of whom Hilary says (*Super Matth.* i) that "they attained the ripe age of eternity through the glory of martyrdom." Therefore martyrdom is not an act of virtue.

From: *Summa Theologiae*, II–II, q. 124, aa. 1–5: "On Martyrdom"

Objection 2. Further, nothing unlawful is an act of virtue. Now it is unlawful to kill oneself, as stated above (II–II, q. 64, a. 5), and yet martyrdom is achieved by so doing: for Augustine says (*De Civ. Dei* i) that "during persecution certain holy women, in order to escape from those who threatened their chastity, threw themselves into a river, and so ended their lives, and their martyrdom is honored in the Catholic Church with most solemn veneration." Therefore martyrdom is not an act of virtue.

Objection 3. Further, it is praiseworthy to offer oneself to do an act of virtue. But it is not praiseworthy to court martyrdom, rather would it seem to be presumptuous and rash. Therefore martyrdom is not an act of virtue.

On the contrary, The reward of beatitude is not due save to acts of virtue. Now it is due to martyrdom, since it is written (Mt. 5:10): "Blessed are they that suffer persecution for justice' sake, for theirs is the kingdom of heaven." Therefore martyrdom is an act of virtue.

I answer that, As stated above (II–II, q. 123, aa. 1 and 3), it belongs to virtue to safeguard man in the good of reason. Now the good of reason consists in the truth as its proper object, and in justice as its proper effect, as shown above (II–II, q. 109, aa. 1 and 2; q. 123, a. 12). And martyrdom consists essentially in standing firmly to truth and justice against the assaults of persecution. Hence it is evident that martyrdom is an act of virtue.

Reply to Objection 1. Some have said that in the case of the Innocents the use of their free will was miraculously accelerated, so that they suffered martyrdom even voluntarily. Since, however, Scripture contains no proof of this, it is better to say that these babes in being slain obtained by God's grace the glory of martyrdom which others acquire by their own will. For the shedding of one's blood for Christ's sake takes the place of Baptism. Wherefore just as in the case of baptized children the merit of Christ is conducive to the acquisition of glory through the baptismal grace, so in those who were slain for Christ's sake the merit of Christ's martyrdom is conducive to the acquisition of the martyr's palm. Hence Augustine says in a sermon on the Epiphany (*De Diversis* lxvi), as though he were addressing them: "A man that does not believe that children are benefited by the baptism of Christ will doubt of your being crowned in suffering for Christ. You were not old enough to believe in Christ's future sufferings, but you had a body wherein you could endure suffering of Christ Who was to suffer."

Reply to Objection 2. Augustine says (*De Civ. Dei* i) that "possibly the Church was induced by certain credible witnesses of Divine authority thus to honor the memory of those holy women."

Reply to Objection 3. The precepts of the Law are about acts of virtue. Now it has been stated (I–II, q. 108, a. 1, ad 4) that some of the precepts of the Divine Law are to be understood in reference to the preparation of the mind, in the sense that man ought to be prepared to do such and such a thing, whenever expedient. On the same way certain things belong to an act of virtue as regards the preparation of the mind, so that in such and such a case a man should act according to reason. And this observation would seem very much to the point in the case of martyrdom, which consists in the right endurance of sufferings unjustly inflicted. Nor ought a man to give another an occasion of acting unjustly: yet if anyone act unjustly, one ought to endure it in moderation.

Article 2: Whether martyrdom is an act of fortitude?

Objection 1. It seems that martyrdom is not an act of fortitude. For the Greek *martyr* signifies a witness. Now witness is borne to the faith of Christ, according to Acts 1:8, "You shall be witnesses unto Me," etc. and Maximus says in a sermon: "The mother of martyrs is the Catholic faith which those glorious warriors have sealed with their blood." Therefore martyrdom is an act of faith rather than of fortitude.

Objection 2. Further, a praiseworthy act belongs chiefly to the virtue which inclines thereto, is manifested thereby, and without which the act avails nothing. Now charity is the chief incentive to martyrdom: Thus Maximus says in a sermon: "The charity of Christ is victorious in His martyrs." Again the greatest proof of charity lies in the act of martyrdom, according to Jn. 15:13, "Greater love than this no man hath, that a man lay down his life for his friends." Moreover without charity martyrdom avails nothing, according to 1 Cor. 13:3, "If I should deliver my body to be burned, and have not charity, it profiteth me nothing." Therefore martyrdom is an act of charity rather than of fortitude.

Objection 3. Further, Augustine says in a sermon on St. Cyprian: "It is easy to honor a martyr by singing his praises, but it is a great thing to imitate his faith and patience." Now that which calls chiefly for praise in a virtuous act, is the virtue of which it is the act. Therefore martyrdom is an act of patience rather than of fortitude.

On the contrary, Cyprian says (*Ep. ad Mart. et Conf.* ii): "Blessed martyrs, with what praise shall I extol you? Most valiant warriors, how shall I find words to proclaim the strength of your courage?" Now a person is praised on account of the virtue whose act he performs. Therefore martyrdom is an act of fortitude.

I answer that, As stated above (II–II, q. 123, a. 1), it belongs to fortitude to strengthen man in the good of virtue, especially against dangers, and chiefly against dangers of death, and most of all against those that occur in battle. Now it is evident that in martyrdom man is firmly strengthened in the good of virtue, since he cleaves to faith and justice notwithstanding the threatening danger of death, the imminence of which is moreover due to a kind of particular contest with his persecutors. Hence Cyprian says in a sermon (*Ep. ad Mart. et Conf.* ii): "The crowd of onlookers wondered to see an unearthly battle, and Christ's servants fighting erect, undaunted in speech, with souls unmoved, and strength divine." Wherefore it is evident that martyrdom is an act of fortitude; for which reason the Church reads in the office of Martyrs: They "became valiant in battle" [Heb. 11:34].

Reply to Objection 1. Two things must be considered in the act of fortitude. One is the good wherein the brave man is strengthened, and this is the end of fortitude; the other is the firmness itself, whereby a man does not yield to the contraries that hinder him from achieving that good, and in this consists the essence of fortitude. Now just as civic fortitude strengthens a man's mind in human justice, for the safeguarding of which he braves the danger of death, so gratuitous fortitude strengthens man's soul in the good of Divine justice, which is "through faith in

Christ Jesus," according to Rm. 3:22. Thus martyrdom is related to faith as the end in which one is strengthened, but to fortitude as the eliciting habit.

Reply to Objection 2. Charity inclines one to the act of martyrdom, as its first and chief motive cause, being the virtue commanding it, whereas fortitude inclines thereto as being its proper motive cause, being the virtue that elicits it. Hence martyrdom is an act of charity as commanding, and of fortitude as eliciting. For this reason also it manifests both virtues. It is due to charity that it is meritorious, like any other act of virtue: and for this reason it avails not without charity.

Reply to Objection 3. As stated above (II–II, q. 123, a. 6), the chief act of fortitude is endurance: to this and not to its secondary act, which is aggression, martyrdom belongs. And since patience serves fortitude on the part of its chief act, viz. endurance, hence it is that martyrs are also praised for their patience.

Article 3: Whether martyrdom is an act of the greatest perfection?

Objection 1. It seems that martyrdom is not an act of the greatest perfection. For seemingly that which is a matter of counsel and not of precept pertains to perfection, because, to wit, it is not necessary for salvation. But it would seem that martyrdom is necessary for salvation, since the Apostle says (Rm. 10:10), "With the heart we believe unto justice, but with the mouth confession is made unto salvation," and it is written (1 Jn. 3:16), that "we ought to lay down our lives for the brethren." Therefore martyrdom does not pertain to perfection.

Objection 2. Further, it seems to point to greater perfection that a man give his soul to God, which is done by obedience, than that he give God his body, which is done by martyrdom: wherefore Gregory says (*Moral.* xxxv) that "obedience is preferable to all sacrifices." Therefore martyrdom is not an act of the greatest perfection.

Objection 3. Further, it would seem better to do good to others than to maintain oneself in good, since the "good of the nation is better than the good of the individual," according to the Philosopher (*Ethic.* i, 2). Now he that suffers martyrdom profits himself alone, whereas he that teaches does good to many. Therefore the act of teaching and guiding subjects is more perfect than the act of martyrdom.

On the contrary, Augustine (*De Sanct. Virgin.* xlvi) prefers martyrdom to virginity which pertains to perfection. Therefore martyrdom seems to belong to perfection in the highest degree.

I answer that, We may speak of an act of virtue in two ways. First, with regard to the species of that act, as compared to the virtue proximately eliciting it. On this way martyrdom, which consists in the due endurance of death, cannot be the most perfect of virtuous acts, because endurance of death is not praiseworthy in itself, but only in so far as it is directed to some good consisting in an act of virtue, such as faith or the love of God, so that this act of virtue being the end is better.

A virtuous act may be considered in another way, in comparison with its first motive cause, which is the love of charity, and it is in this respect that an act comes to belong to the perfection of life, since, as the Apostle says (Col. 3:14), "charity ... is the bond of perfection." Now, of all virtuous acts martyrdom is the greatest proof of the perfection of charity: since a man's love for a thing is proved to be so much the greater, according as that which he despises for its sake is more dear to him, or that which he chooses to suffer for its sake is more odious. But it is evident that of all the goods of the present life man loves life itself most, and on the other hand he hates death more than anything, especially when it is accompanied by the pains of bodily torment, "from fear of which even dumb animals refrain from the greatest pleasures," as Augustine observes (Q. 83, q. 36). And from this point of view it is clear that martyrdom is the most perfect of human acts in respect of its genus, as being the sign of the greatest charity, according to Jn. 15:13: "Greater love than this no man hath, that a man lay down his life for his friends."

Reply to Objection 1. There is no act of perfection, which is a matter of counsel, but what in certain cases is a matter of precept, as being necessary for salvation. Thus Augustine declares (*De Adult. Conjug.* xiii) that a man is under the obligation of observing continence, through the absence or sickness of his wife. Hence it is not contrary to the perfection of martyrdom if in certain cases it be necessary for salvation, since there are cases when it is not necessary for salvation to suffer martyrdom; thus we read of many holy martyrs who through zeal for the faith or brotherly love gave themselves up to martyrdom of their own accord. As to these precepts, they are to be understood as referring to the preparation of the mind.

Reply to Objection 2. Martyrdom embraces the highest possible degree of obedience, namely obedience unto death; thus we read of Christ (Phil. 2:8) that He became "obedient unto death." Hence it is evident that martyrdom is of itself more perfect than obedience considered absolutely.

Reply to Objection 3. This argument considers martyrdom according to the proper species of its act, whence it derives no excellence over all other virtuous acts; thus neither is fortitude more excellent than all virtues.

Article 4: Whether death is essential to martyrdom?

Objection 1. It seems that death is not essential to martyrdom. For Jerome says in a sermon on the Assumption (*Epist. ad Paul. et Eustoch.*): "I should say rightly that the Mother of God was both virgin and martyr, although she ended her days in peace": and Gregory says (*Hom.* iii *in Evang.*): "Although persecution has ceased to offer the opportunity, yet the peace we enjoy is not without its martyrdom, since even if we no longer yield the life of the body to the sword, yet do we slay fleshly desires in the soul with the sword of the spirit." Therefore there can be martyrdom without suffering death.

Objection 2. Further, we read of certain women as commended for despising life for the sake of safeguarding the integrity of the flesh: wherefore seemingly the integrity of chastity is preferable to the life of the body. Now sometimes the integrity of the flesh has been forfeited or has been threatened in confession of the Christian faith, as in the case of Agnes and Lucy. Therefore it seems that the name of martyr should be accorded to a woman who forfeits the integrity of the flesh for the sake of Christ's faith, rather than if she were to forfeit even the life of the body: wherefore also Lucy said: "If thou causest me to be violated against my will, my chastity will gain me a twofold crown."

Objection 3. Further, martyrdom is an act of fortitude. But it belongs to fortitude to brave not only death but also other hardships, as Augustine declares (*Music.* vi). Now there are many other hardships besides death, which one may suffer for Christ's faith, namely imprisonment, exile, being stripped of one's goods, as mentioned in Heb. 10:34, for which reason we celebrate the martyrdom of Pope Saint Marcellus, notwithstanding that he died in prison. Therefore it is not essential to martyrdom that one suffer the pain of death.

Objection 4. Further, martyrdom is a meritorious act, as stated above (II–II, q. 124, a. 2, ad 1; a. 3). Now it cannot be a meritorious act after death. Therefore it is before death; and consequently death is not essential to martyrdom.

On the contrary, Maximus says in a sermon on the martyrs that "in dying for the faith he conquers who would have been vanquished in living without faith."

I answer that As stated above (II–II, q. 124, a. 2), a martyr is so called as being a witness to the Christian faith, which teaches us to despise things visible for the sake of things invisible, as stated in Heb. 11. Accordingly it belongs to martyrdom that a man bear witness to the faith in showing by deed that he despises all things present, in order to obtain invisible goods to come. Now so long as a man retains the life of the body he does not show by deed that he despises all things relating to the body. For men are wont to despise both their kindred and all they possess, and even to suffer bodily pain, rather than lose life. Hence Satan testified against Job (Job 2:4): "Skin for skin, and all that a man hath he will give for his soul," i.e. for the life of his body. Therefore the perfect notion of martyrdom requires that a man suffer death for Christ's sake.

Reply to Objection 1. The authorities quoted, and the like that one may meet with, speak of martyrdom by way of similitude.

Reply to Objection 2. When a woman forfeits the integrity of the flesh, or is condemned to forfeit it under pretext of the Christian faith, it is not evident to men whether she suffers this for love of the Christian faith, or rather through contempt of chastity. Wherefore in the sight of men her testimony is not held to be sufficient, and consequently this is not martyrdom properly speaking. In the sight of God, however, Who searcheth the heart, this may be deemed worthy of a reward, as Lucy said.

Reply to Objection 3. As stated above (II–II, q. 123, aa. 4, 5), fortitude regards danger of death chiefly, and other dangers consequently; wherefore a person is not called a martyr merely for suffering imprisonment, or exile, or forfeiture of his wealth, except in so far as these result in death.

Reply to Objection 4. The merit of martyrdom is not after death, but in the voluntary endurance of death, namely in the fact that a person willingly suffers being put to death. It happens sometimes, however, that a man lives for some time after being mortally wounded for Christ's sake, or after suffering for the faith of Christ any other kind of hardship inflicted by persecution and continued until death ensues. The act of martyrdom is meritorious while a man is in this state, and at the very time that he is suffering these hardships.

Article 5: Whether faith alone is the cause of martyrdom?

Objection 1. It seems that faith alone is the cause of martyrdom. For it is written (1 Pt. 4:15,16): "Let none of you suffer as a murderer, or a thief, or a railer, or a coveter of other men's things. But if as a Christian, let him not be ashamed, but let him glorify God in this name." Now a man is said to be a Christian because he holds the faith of Christ. Therefore only faith in Christ gives the glory of martyrdom to those who suffer.

Objection 2. Further, a martyr is a kind of witness. But witness is borne to the truth alone. Now one is not called a martyr for bearing witness to any truth, but only for witnessing to the Divine truth, otherwise a man would be a martyr if he were to die for confessing a truth of geometry or some other speculative science, which seems ridiculous. Therefore faith alone is the cause of martyrdom.

Objection 3. Further, those virtuous deeds would seem to be of most account which are directed to the common good, since "the good of the nation is better than the good of the individual," according to the Philosopher (*Ethic.* i, 2). If, then, some other good were the cause of martyrdom, it would seem that before all those would be martyrs who die for the defense of their country. Yet this is not consistent with Church observance, for we do not celebrate the martyrdom of those who die in a just war. Therefore faith alone is the cause of martyrdom.

On the contrary, It is written (Mt. 5:10): "Blessed are they that suffer persecution for justice' sake," which pertains to martyrdom, according to a gloss, as well as Jerome's commentary on this passage. Now not only faith but also the other virtues pertain to justice. Therefore other virtues can be the cause of martyrdom.

I answer that, As stated above (II–II, q. 124, a. 4), martyrs are so called as being witnesses, because by suffering in body unto death they bear witness to the truth; not indeed to any truth, but to the truth which is in accordance with godliness, and was made known to us by Christ: wherefore Christ's martyrs are His witnesses. Now this truth is the truth of faith. Wherefore the cause of all martyrdom is the truth of faith.

But the truth of faith includes not only inward belief, but also outward profession, which is expressed not only by words, whereby one confesses the faith, but also by deeds, whereby a person shows that he has faith, according to James 2:18, "I will show thee, by works, my faith." Hence it is written of certain people (Titus 1:16): "They profess that they know God but in their works they deny Him." Thus all virtuous deeds, inasmuch as they are referred to God, are professions of the faith whereby we come to know that God requires these works of us, and rewards us for them: and in this way they can be the cause of martyrdom. For this reason the Church celebrates the martyrdom of blessed John the Baptist, who suffered death, not for refusing to deny the faith, but for reproving adultery.

Reply to Objection 1. A Christian is one who is Christ's. Now a person is said to be Christ's, not only through having faith in Christ, but also because he is actuated to virtuous deeds by the Spirit of Christ, according to Rm. 8:9, "If any man have not the Spirit of Christ, he is none of His"; and again because in imitation of Christ he is dead to sins, according to Gal. 5:24, "They that are Christ's have crucified their flesh with the vices and concupiscences." Hence to suffer as a Christian is not only to suffer in confession of the faith, which is done by words, but also to suffer for doing any good work, or for avoiding any sin, for Christ's sake, because this all comes under the head of witnessing to the faith.

Reply to Objection 2. The truth of other sciences has no connection with the worship of the Godhead: hence it is not called truth according to godliness, and consequently the confession thereof cannot be said to be the direct cause of martyrdom. Yet, since every lie is a sin, as stated above (II–II, q. 110, aa. 3, 4), avoidance of a lie, to whatever truth it may be contrary, may be the cause of martyrdom inasmuch as a lie is a sin against the Divine Law.

Reply to Objection 3. The good of one's country is paramount among human goods: yet the Divine good, which is the proper cause of martyrdom, is of more account than human good. Nevertheless, since human good may become Divine, for instance when it is referred to God, it follows that any human good in so far as it is referred to God, may be the cause of martyrdom.

Questions for St. Thomas Aquinas

1. If it is unlawful to kill oneself, why is martyrdom praiseworthy?
2. In what way is martyrdom a "witnessing"?
3. Why is martyrdom "the greatest proof of the perfection of charity"?

St. Catherine of Siena

Few saints are as beloved as St. Catherine of Siena (1347–1380), who is universally recognized as one of the greatest Doctors (or Teachers) of the Church. In her mystical *Dialogue* with God, composed shortly before her death at the age of 33, St. Catherine reminds us that wealth is an impediment to holy dying. Human beings tend to cling to material possessions, to worldly status, to accomplishments; but in the eyes of God, *nothing* is of value except for love.

MY TRUTH SAID IN THE HOLY GOSPEL that it is more impossible for a rich person to enter eternal life than for a camel to pass through the eye of a needle. Such are those who possess or desire wealth with miserably disordered affection. For there are many who are poor, as I have told you, who by their disordered affection possess the whole world with their will if only they could have it. They cannot pass through the gate because it is narrow and low. Only if they throw their load to the ground and restrain their affection for the world and bow their head in humility will they be able to pass through. And there is no other gate but this that leads to eternal life.

The gate is broad that leads to eternal damnation, and blind as they are it seems they do not see their own destruction, for even in this life

Excerpts from *Catherine of Siena: The Dialogue*, pp. 318–324, translation and introduction by Suzanne Noffke, O.P., from The Classics of Western Spirituality Series, Copyright © 1980 by Paulist Press, Inc., New York / Mahwah, NJ. Used with permission of Paulist Press, www.paulistpress.com.

they have a foretaste of hell. They are always suffering because they are wanting more than they can have. They suffer over what they do not have, and what they lose they lose with grief. Their grief is as great as was their love in possessing. They lose all affection for their neighbors and have no care for acquiring virtue.

O rottenness of the world! Not the things of the world in themselves, because I created everything good and perfect. But rotten are those who seek and keep these things with disordered love.

Dearest daughter, your tongue could never tell how many are the evils that come from this. They see and experience them every day, but they do not want to see or recognize their harmfulness.

I have touched on these few things because I want you to know better the treasure of spiritually motivated voluntary poverty. Who knows it? My beloved poor servants who in order to be able to travel this road and enter through this narrow gate have thrown to the ground the burden of riches.

Some throw it down both in fact and in spirit: These are those who observe both the commandments and the counsels in fact as well as in spirit. The others observe the counsels in spirit only, stripping themselves of attachment to wealth, so that they do not possess it with disordered love but with holy fear. In fact, they are not so much possessors of it as distributors for the poor. This is good, but the first way is perfect, more fruitful and less encumbered, and there my providence is more clearly reflected in actuality. (I will finish telling you about this when I am speaking in praise of true poverty.) Both the one and the other bow their heads, making themselves small in true humility. But because I have told you elsewhere about the second—if you remember well, I did tell you something about it—I will now tell you only about the first.

I have shown you how every evil, harm, and suffering, in this life and in the next, comes from selfish love of riches.

Now, on the opposite side, I am telling you that every good, peace, rest, and calm comes from poverty. Only look at the faces of those who are truly poor: how happy and joyful they are! The only thing that saddens them is when I am offended, and this sadness fattens rather than distresses the soul. Through poverty they have gained the highest of riches. By leaving darkness behind they discover the most perfect light for themselves. By leaving behind worldly sadness they have come to possess happiness. In place of mortal goods they find the immortal. The greatest of consolations is theirs. Their labors and suffering are refreshment to them. They are just and love everyone with a familial love. They do not play favorites.

In whom do the virtues of most holy faith and true hope shine forth? Where does the fire of divine charity burn? In those who, by the light of their faith in me, supreme eternal wealth, raise their hope above the world and above all empty riches to embrace true poverty as their bride along with her servants. And do you know what these servants of poverty are? Contempt for oneself and true humility, which serve and nurture the soul's love for poverty. With this faith and hope, ablaze with the fire of charity, my true servants leaped and leap above riches and selfishness. Just so, the glorious apostle Matthew leaped up from his tax booth and, leaving his great wealth behind, followed my Truth, who taught you the way and the rule by teaching you to love and follow this poverty. And he taught you not only with words but by his example as well, from his birth right up to the end of his life. For you he took poverty as his bride, though he was wealth itself by his union with the divine nature, for he is one thing with me and I with him, eternal wealth.

And if you would see him humiliated and in great poverty, look at God made man, clothed in the lowliness of your humanity.

You see this gentle loving Word born in a stable while Mary was on a journey, to show you pilgrims how you should be constantly born anew in the stable of self-knowledge, where by grace you will find me born within your soul. You see him lying among the animals, in such poverty that Mary had nothing to cover him up with. It was winter, and she kept him warm with the animals' breath and a blanket of hay. He is the fire of charity but he chose to endure the cold in his humanity.

All the while he lived he chose to suffer, whether his disciples joined him or not, as when once because of their hunger the disciples plucked ears of corn and ate the grain.

At the end of his life, stripped naked, scourged at the pillar, parched with thirst, he was so poor on the wood of the cross that neither the earth nor the wood could give him a place to lay his head. He had nowhere to rest it except on his own shoulder. And drunk as he was with love, he made a bath for you of his blood when this Lamb's body was broken open and bled from every part.

Out of his misery he gave you great wealth. From the narrow wood of the cross he extended his generosity to everyone. By tasting the bitterness of the gall he gave you the most perfect sweetness. From his sadness he gave you consolation. He was nailed to the cross to loose you from the chains of deadly sin. By becoming a servant he rescued you from slavery to the devil and set you free. He was sold to ransom you with his blood. By choosing death for himself he gave you life.

How truly, then, has he given you love as your rule by showing you more love than you could ever show, giving his life for you who were enemies to him and to me the high eternal Father. The foolish ones who so offend me and scorn the great price he paid do not recognize this. He gave you true humility as your rule by humbling himself in his shameful death on the cross. He gave you lowliness as your rule by suffering such disgrace and great reproach. And he gave you true poverty as your rule, for Scripture laments in his name, "The foxes have dens, the birds have nests, but the Virgin's Son has nowhere to lay his head." Who knows this? Those who are enlightened by most holy faith. In whom do you find this faith? In the spiritually poor who have taken as their bride Queen Poverty, for they have cast away the riches that bring on the darkness of infidelity.

This queen's realm is never at war, but is always peaceful and calm. She overflows with justice, because the thing that perpetrates injustice is cut off from her. Her city walls are strong, because their foundation is not in the earth, nor on the sand that every little wind scares up from the earth, but on the living rock, the gentle Christ Jesus my only-begotten Son. There is no darkness within her, but fire without any cold, because this queen's mother is divine charity. This city's adornment is compassion and mercy, because the cruel tyrant wealth has been put out. There is benevolence, that is, neighborly affection, among all its citizens. There is enduring perseverance and prudence, for poverty does not act or govern her city imprudently but watches over it with great concern and prudence. Thus the soul who takes this gentle queen, poverty, as bride is made master of all these riches, for the two go hand in hand. The only condition is that the plague of hankering after wealth not come upon that soul, for then she would be cut off from that good and find herself outside the city in the greatest misery. But if she is loyal and faithful to this bride, she will bestow her wealth on her forever and ever.

Who sees such excellence? The soul in whom the light of faith is shining. This bride clothes her spouse anew in purity by taking away the wealth that had made her unclean. She deprives her of wicked companions and gives her good ones instead. She drains out from her the pus of carelessness by casting out care for the world and riches. She draws out what is bitter and leaves what is sweet; she pulls out the thorns and leaves the rose. She empties the soul's stomach of the rotten humors of disordered love and makes it light, and as soon as it is emptied she fills it with the food of virtues that bring the greatest sweetness. She gives the soul hatred and love as servants so that she will clean her dwelling place. Thus hatred for vice and selfish sensuality sweep out the soul, and love for virtue adorns her. She relieves her of all doubt by taking away her slavish fear and gives her confidence and holy fear instead.

    The soul who takes Queen Poverty as bride finds all the virtues, all the graces and pleasures and delights she could desire more. She has no fear of vexation, for no one is at war against her. She has no fear of hunger or want, because her faith sees and trusts me, her Creator and the source of all wealth and providence, for I always feed and nurture her. Have you ever found a servant of mine, a spouse of poverty, who died of hunger? No. There have been some who had great and overflowing riches and have perished because they trusted in their riches rather than in me. But I never fail those who never fail in their hope. I provide for them as a kind compassionate father. And with what glad generosity they come to me, because they have come to know by the light of faith that my providence always has and always will provide for every spiritual and temporal need. True, I let them suffer to make them grow in faith and hope and so that I may reward them for their labors, but I never fail to give them anything they need. In everything they sweetly experience the depth of my providence, tasting in it the milk of divine tenderness, and this is why they do not fear the bitterness of death. Rather they run on with eager longing, dead as they are to selfish feelings about themselves and riches, arm in arm with poverty their bride. They are people in love and alive in my will, ready to endure heat, cold, and nakedness, hunger and thirst, anguish and abuse and even death, in their desire to give their life for love of Life (that is, for me, for I am their life), and to shed their blood for love of the blood.

    Look at the poor apostles and the other glorious martyrs, Peter, Paul, Stephen. Look at Lawrence, who seemed to be not over the fire but over the most pleasant of flowers, joking, as it were, with the tyrant and saying, "This side is cooked; turn it over and start eating!" The fire of divine charity was so great that in his soul's feeling he regarded the lesser fire as nothing. And to Stephen the stones seemed like roses. What was the reason? The love with which he had taken true and perfect poverty as his bride. He had left the world behind for the glory and praise of my name and espoused poverty by the light of most holy faith with firm trust and ready obedience. These souls became obedient both in fact and in spirit to the commandments and to the counsels given them by my Truth.

They are desirous of death and scornful and impatient of life, not because they wish to escape toil and weariness, but because they want to be united with me, their end. And why are they not afraid of death as people naturally are? Because poverty their bride has made them secure by taking away their attachment to themselves and to riches. Thus, with virtue they have trampled their natural love underfoot and have received this divine light and love that are beyond nature. How could those in such a state be sad about death? For their desire is to leave this life behind, and it pains them to see it so prolonged. Could those who have so eagerly spurned worldly pleasures and riches be sorry to leave them behind? It is not surprising, for one who does not love is not sad; indeed, it is a pleasure to leave behind what one hates. So wherever you turn you find in these souls perfect peace and calm and every good thing. And in the wicked who possess things with such disordered love you see the greatest evil and unbearable suffering. Even though on the outside they may seem the opposite, in truth it is always so.

Who would not have judged that poor Lazarus was supremely miserable and the rich man quite happy and content? Yet such was not the case, for that rich man with all his wealth suffered more than poor Lazarus tormented by his leprosy. For the rich man's [selfish] will was alive, and this is the source of all suffering. But in Lazarus this will was dead and his will was so alive in me that he found refreshment and consolation in his pain. He had been thrown out by others, especially by the rich man, and was neither cleansed nor cared for by them, but I provided that the senseless animals should lick his sores. And you see how at the end of their lives Lazarus has eternal life and the rich man is in hell.

So the rich are left sad while my poor are happy. I hold them to my breast and give them the milk of great consolation. Because they leave everything they possess me completely. The Holy Spirit becomes the nurse of their souls and their little bodies in every situation. I make the animals provide for them in this way and that, depending on their need.

If a hermit is ill I make another hermit leave his cell to help him. You know how often I have pulled you out of your cell to satisfy the needs of the poor. Sometimes I have let you experience this yourself by using this same kind of providence to help you when you were in need, and even when creatures failed you, I your Creator did not. In every way I provide for [my poor]. How does it happen that people who have wealth and take such good care of their bodies and have so many clothes are always sickly—and then when they come to despise themselves and embrace poverty with just enough clothes to cover their bodies they become strong and healthy and it seems nothing can hurt them, that neither cold nor heat nor coarse foods can harm their body? My providence is the reason, for I provide and deprive and care for those who completely surrender themselves.

So you see, most beloved daughter, how great is the contentment and delight of these beloved poor of mine.

Questions for St. Catherine of Siena

1. What kind of poverty will we need in order to learn how to die?
2. Meditate about how our possessions and privileges increase our fear of death.
3. Describe the state of detachment that is "Queen Poverty."

St. Catherine of Genoa

Active during the years just preceding the Reformation, St. Catherine of Genoa (1447–1510) was a married laywoman and a contemplative mystic, who in addition to her writings devoted her adult years to active service of the poor and the sick. One of her followers composed this account of her dying. In the description of the intense pain she endured, and the presence of God nourishing her spirit to enable her to endure this pain and prepare for eternal life, we can see how, if we allow him, God will be present in the midst of our dying.

THIS BLESSED SOUL walked the ways of God for some thirty-five years, with remarkable inner experiences, in a long succession of days, weeks, and months of a suffering that culminated in a happy death.

The night of the feast of St. Lawrence, it seemed that her body was on fire like that of the saint, for it thrashed about in all directions. On the following day, since her body was still in extreme pain, God visited her and drew her to Him. Catherine remained with her eyes fixed on the ceiling and did not move for an hour. Though she did not move or speak, she laughed with great joy.

Excerpts from *Catherine of Genoa: Purgation and Purgatory: The Spiritual Dialogue*, pp. 140–148, from The Classics of Western Spirituality Series, translated with notes by Serge Hughes, Copyright © 1979, Paulist Press, Inc., New York / Mahwah, NJ. Used with permission of Paulist Press, www.paulistpress.com.

When she came back to herself, she was asked what she had seen. She answered that God had shown her a spark of the joys of eternal life and that that had made her laugh out of sheer joy.

And all she said was: "O Lord, do with me what You will." This was a sign that she was approaching the end.

On August 14, the vigil of the feast of the Assumption, she was in great travail day and night, and it was thought that she was about to die. When she was about to receive Communion at the usual time, she spoke such loving words to the Sacrament that many present wept. In the presence of the Blessed Sacrament she was often passionately inspired, for her great and unutterable love for it penetrated to the deepest part of herself.

The subsequent day and night she was in great pain, and again many thought that she was about to die. She asked for Extreme Unction, which was given to her and which she received with great devotion.

The next day she was jubilant and laughed out loud. She thought she saw a divine face, which gave her immense joy. Those around her looked about but could not understand what made her so happy. When the vision disappeared she was asked what she had seen. She answered that she had seen extremely beautiful faces, happy and mirthful, and could not but rejoice with them.

This joy lasted for seven days, during which she seemed much improved, a truly supernatural phenomenon in the sudden passing from death to life.

On the vigil of St. Bartholomew, again as several times before, it seemed that she was about to die. She was twenty-four hours without food and if she took some she could not keep it on her stomach. At about seven o'clock in the evening she had a diabolical vision that assaulted her body and soul. Unable to speak, she motioned to them to make the sign of the cross above her heart, and she crossed herself, though it was difficult to make out what she was saying. Only later was it clear that she had been subjected to a diabolical temptation.

She beckoned to them to bring surplices, stoles, and holy water to her. This was done and in half an hour she felt liberated. Once more herself, she said that God had allowed her to be subjected to that temptation. And since she was so burning within with the fire of divine love, she felt such repugnance for that vision that she would gladly have hurled herself into hell rather than long endure that temptation. She was not shown sins she had ever committed, for that would have been much worse than the diabolical vision.

On the twenty-fifth of August she was so weak that she could barely keep her eyes open. She had them open the window so that she could see the sky. Later in the evening she had them light candles. As the candles were burning, she sang as well as she could the "Veni Creator Spiritus," and others accompanied her. When she had finished singing she looked up to heaven and remained thus for about an hour and a half. She moved her hands and eyes a great deal, which puzzled those standing by her, who wondered what she might be seeing, since she seemed so intensely happy that it appeared she would die of joy. When she came back to herself she said many times, "Let us leave, let us leave." And then she said, "No more of this world, no more of this world." The memory of that vision left her all broken so that she could neither speak nor move.

On the twenty-seventh of the month she saw herself without body and without soul, as she had always wished to be; that is, with her spirit completely in God, and having lost sight of heaven and earth, as if she no longer existed.

She saw this vision so clearly and felt so stripped down to her bare being that she had all leave her room and asked that only those who had to should come in. She had no dealings with any creature except out of pure necessity, nor did she want anyone to speak to her unless they had a compelling reason. She was so absorbed within that her humanity could not be concerned with any earthly thing. For two days she remained thus. It seemed as if she could find no rest and was quite out of herself.

On the next day, the twenty-eighth, she had a very hard day and night. Some four months before it seemed that on feast days, especially on those of the apostles, martyrs, and Our Lord, she felt more pain than on other days. Because of that inner fire she became as yellow as saffron, a sign that the inner fire was consuming her humanity.

On September 2 she seemed utterly without strength. She tried to take something, but it made matters worse, because of the efforts she had to make; and this happened several times. There was no way to help her.

She spoke only rarely, utterly drained of strength, burning with that inner fire without being able to drink as much as a drop of water. She easily swallowed the Communion wafer, however, and said that it was no sooner in her mouth than it was in her heart. Nor could she take any other food, for it would not stay down. At this point the doctors said that there was no point in forcing her to eat, that it only made matters worse, as she herself had insisted.

The following day, in great pain, she stretched out her arms so that she looked like a body nailed to the cross, her appearance reflecting her inner crucifixion. And she said: "Let every suffering and pain be welcome that comes from God's will, for you have illuminated me, O Lord, for the last thirty-six years or so. For your sake I have always sought to suffer, within as well as without. And this desire has never let me suffer greatly. On the contrary, all those things that I have undergone that seemed intense suffering were, because of your will, sweet and consoling. Now that I am at the end and seem to be in such pain from head to toe that it would seem that the body could not endure it and would be about to die and be quite annihilated, I see that you who rule over all things with your will do not want me to die as yet. So that in the midst of the pain my body endures, without comfort of any kind, I still cannot say that I am suffering. You make all things bearable, and my joy is such that it cannot be imagined or expressed." As was her wont, on September 5 she received Communion. At the very moment she had a vision of a dead woman on a bier, accompanied by many religious dressed in black, and this vision gave her an immense joy; and she spoke of it to her confessor as if she had some scruples over such joy. The inner fire was intensifying and making her so weak that she could no longer move.

On September 6 a new nail was driven into her heart, which caused her great pain and lasted about ten hours. She would cry aloud, especially when she would abruptly wake from her sleep, which was not sleep, although it resembled it for she was so weak and exhausted that she seemed dead; and this happened because of the inner fire.

On September 7 she received Communion, observing the fast, without eating or drinking. In the twentieth hour she felt such joy that she could not but smile continuously for about two hours.

After this, she saw a ray of divine love that was almost unbearable and that burned up her humanity, which could not defend itself, given its frailty.

She then saw a ladder of flame and felt herself drawn upwards, experiencing great joy therein. This vision lasted for about four hours.

Because of the intense fire in which that humanity was being consumed, she asked those present to open the window to see whether the world was on fire. She was sure that was the case; and this showed that she was right in saying to her humanity that it would have been better off in a burning furnace than in that spiritual fire through which it had to pass to completely annihilate its nature.

On the eighth day of the month she received Communion in the usual way, remaining for all of those days without eating or drinking.

The following day she again received Communion in the same way. And in a vision she saw many of the wretched parts of her life, and that greatly distressed her. When she could speak of them she did, and then the distress left her. They were things of no importance, but for her the least defect was intolerable.

She then had the experience of a pure soul, incapable of any memory but those of things divine. And on contemplating this state she smiled and said, "Oh, who could ever be worthy of all this!" She so marveled at this vision that for a long time she seemed motionless and abstracted from all things.

A short time thereafter she saw another ray of divine fire, which gladdened her, but she could not express what she felt. Those near her, however, could tell that she was closer to heaven than to earth.

On the tenth she received Communion as usual, without having eaten or drunk, but the inner fire continued to rage.

In these days ten doctors gathered together to see whether they could help her in any way with their skills. On examining her, they concluded that her case was not a normal sickness but a supernatural one, for neither her pulse, urine, nor any other sign showed a bodily illness. And marveling, and asking her for her prayers, they left.

The fire was so intense that day that she felt she was reduced to ashes. If they put water in her mouth she would immediately spit it out and not a drop of it would be swallowed. All marveled at how she could continue to live without eating or drinking, and suffering so.

As for her clarity of mind, her speech, her pulse, all was normal (that is, when she was not so weak that she could not talk), but when she appeared to be suffocating she looked quite dead; and then abruptly she would come to again. This was evidently the working of God, and all marveled.

On the twelfth, she received Communion, as was customary. She remained for a while without talking and then, wetting her lips, she said, "I am drowning!" For a drop of water had gone down her throat and she could not swallow it. She did not talk or open her eyes for the rest of that day. At night, at the tenth hour, she complained of the fire and vomited some black clotted blood. There were also black blotches all over her body and in her weakness and suffering she could not recognize any of those who stood around her.

On the thirteenth, at the twenty-third hour, she vomited a great deal of blood, and that continued all night, so that she was extremely weak. At the usual hour she received Communion. On seeing the blood, so hot that basins in which it was gathered were burning, those present marveled that she could continue to live and felt that truly there was a fire in her. Then Catherine looked up at the ceiling, gesturing with her hands and trying to speak. Those present asked her what she wanted and she said, "Drive away that beast, who wants to eat!" and that was all they could make out.

On the fourteenth she again vomited much blood. Her pulse was barely audible, as fine as a hair, and often they could not find it. Nonetheless, she spoke clearly and strongly and that night, as usual, she received Communion.

She spent all of that day and the following night in the same condition until the sixth hour, at which time she was surrounded by many of her devoted followers, who witnessed all of these things.

She was then asked if she wanted to receive Communion. She answered by asking whether it was the usual time, and then pointed her finger toward heaven. The gesture implied that she was to receive Communion in heaven, where she would be perpetually united to that sweet Sacrament and her loving God.

Thus in that very hour, in all peace and tranquility, she gently left this life and went to her sweet love, whom she now sees and takes joy in for all time. Until the very last she was clear in mind, and did not remain silent for more than a half hour.

Questions for St. Catherine of Genoa

1. How does St. Catherine's experience of a feeling of "spiritual nakedness" assist her dying?
2. What is the role of the sacrament of the Eucharist in St. Catherine's process of dying?
3. How might her suffering inform our own understanding of the suffering that we (or our loved ones) might undergo in dying?

St. Thomas More, Part I

While imprisoned in the Tower of London, where he was sentenced to death for refusing to acknowledge Henry VIII's supremacy over the Church in England, St. Thomas More (1478–1535) spent much of his time writing. A prolific and brilliant author, and a leading politician who had risen to the rank of Chancellor, he prepared for his execution especially by meditating upon Christ's last hours. Christ did not hide his sorrow, but neither did Christ allow his sorrow to lead him to deny the truth in order to avoid suffering. In the following two excerpts from More's writings, we see how he places himself firmly into God's hands.

AND HE SAID, "Sit down here while I go over there to pray." And He took Peter and the two sons of Zebedee with Him. He began to feel sorrow and grief and fear and weariness. Then He said to them, "My soul is sad unto death. Stay here and keep watch with me." (Mt 26:36–38, Mk 14:32–34)

Commanding the other eight to stop somewhat lower down, He went further on, taking with Him Peter, John, and his brother James, the three whom He had always singled out from the rest of the apostles by a certain special privilege of intimacy. Now even if He had done this for no other reason than that He wanted to, no one ought to have been envious

From: Thomas More, *The Sadness of Christ*, trans. Clarence Miller, ed. Gerard Wegemer (Princeton, NJ: Scepter, 1993), pp. 6–17. Used by permission of Yale University Press.

because of His generosity. But still there were certain reasons for this which He might well have had in mind. For Peter was outstanding for his zealous faith and John for his virginity, and his brother James was to be the very first of all to suffer martyrdom in the name of Christ. Furthermore, these were the three to whom He had formerly granted the secret knowledge and open sight of His glorified body. It was only right, then, that those same three whom He had admitted to such an extraordinary vision, and whom He had invigorated with a momentary flash of the eternal brilliance so that they ought to have been stronger than the others, should have assigned to them the role of His nearest supporters in the preliminary agony of His passion. But when He had gone on a little way, He suddenly felt such a sharp and bitter attack of sadness, grief, fear, and weariness that He immediately uttered, even in their presence, those anguished words which gave expression to His overburdened feelings: "My soul is sad unto death."

For a huge mass of troubles took possession of the tender and gentle body of our most holy Savior. He knew that His ordeal was now imminent and just about to overtake Him: the treacherous betrayer, the bitter enemies, binding ropes, false accusations, slanders, blows, thorns, nails, the cross, and horrible tortures stretched out over many hours. Over and above these, He was tormented by the thought of His disciples' terror, and loss of the Jews, even the destruction of the very man who so disloyally betrayed Him, and finally the ineffable grief of His beloved mother. The gathered storm of all these evils rushed into His most gentle heart and flooded it like the ocean sweeping through broken dikes.

Perhaps someone may wonder how it could be that our Savior Christ could feel sadness, sorrow, and grief, since He was truly God, equal to His all-powerful Father. Certainly He could not have felt them if He had been God (as He was) in such a way as not to be man also. But as a matter of face, since He was no less really a man than He was really God, I see no reason for us to be surprised that insofar as He was man, He had the ordinary feelings of mankind (though certainly no blameworthy ones)—no more than we would be surprised that insofar as He was God, He performed stupendous miracles. For if we are surprised that Christ felt fear, weariness, and grief, simply on the grounds that He was God, why should we not also be surprised that He experienced hunger, thirst, and sleep, seeing that He was none the less divine for doing these things? But here, perhaps, you may object, "I am no longer surprised at

His capacity for these emotions, but I cannot help being surprised at His desire to experience them. For He taught His disciples not to be afraid of those who can kill the body only and can do nothing beyond that; and how can it be fitting that He Himself should now be very much afraid of those same persons, especially since even His body could suffer nothing from them except that He Himself allowed?

"Furthermore, since we know His martyrs rushed to their deaths eagerly and joyfully, triumphing over tyrants and torturers, how can it not seem inappropriate that Christ Himself, the very prototype and leader of martyrs, the standard-bearer of them all, should be so terrified at the approach of pain, so shaken, so utterly downcast? Shouldn't He rather have been especially careful to set a good example in this manner, just as He had always let His deeds precede His precepts, so that others might learn from His own example to undergo death eagerly for truth's sake and so that those who afterwards would suffer death for the faith with fear and hesitation might now indulge their slackness by imagining that they are following Christ's precedent?—whereas actually their reluctance would both detract a great deal from the glory of their cause and discourage others who observe their sadness and fear." Those who bring up these objections and others of the same sort do not scrutinize carefully enough all the facets of this problem and do not pay enough attention to what Christ meant when He forbade His followers to fear death. For He hardly intended it to mean that they should never under any circumstances recoil from a violent death, but rather that they should not, out of fear, flee from a death which will not last, only to run, by denying the faith, into one which will be everlasting. For He wished His followers to be brave and prudent soldiers, not senseless and foolish. The brave man bears up under the blows which beset him; the senseless man simply does not feel them when they strike. Only a foolish man does not fear wounds, but a prudent man does not allow any fear of suffering to divert him from a holy way of life, for that would be to refuse lesser pains at the expense of plunging himself into far more bitter ones.

When an afflicted part of the body is to be cut or cauterized, the doctor does not try to persuade the sick man not to feel any mental anguish at the thought of the pain the cutting or burning will cause, but rather encourages him to bear up under it. He admits it will be painful, but stresses that the pain will be outweighed by the pleasure of health and the avoidance of even more horrible pain. Indeed, though our Savior

Christ commands us to suffer death (when it cannot be avoided) rather than fall away from him through a fear of death (and we do all fall away from Him when we publicly deny our faith in Him), still He is so far from requiring us to do violence to our nature by not fearing death at all that He even leaves us free to flee from punishment (whenever this can be done without injury to His cause). "If you are persecuted in one city," He says, "flee to another" (Mt 10:23). This permission, this cautious advice of a prudent master, was followed by almost all the apostles and by almost all the illustrious martyrs in the many succeeding centuries: there is hardly one of them who did not use it at some time or other to save his life and extend it, with great profit to himself and others, until such a time as the hidden providence of God foresaw was more fitting.

On the other hand, some brave champions have taken the initiative by publicly professing their Christianity, though no one was trying to discover it, and by freely exposing themselves to death, though no one was demanding it. Thus God chose, according to His pleasure, to increase His glory sometimes by concealing the riches of the faith, so that those who set clever traps for His believers might be duped, sometimes by displaying them, so that those who cruelly persecuted His followers might be incensed by seeing all their hopes frustrated and finding, much to their outrage, that all their ferocity could not overcome martyrs who met death willingly. But God in His mercy does not command us to climb this steep and lofty peak of bravery, and hence it is not safe for just anyone to go rushing on heedlessly to the point where he cannot retrace his steps gradually but may be in danger of falling head over heels into the abyss if he cannot make it to the summit. As for those whom God calls to do this, let them choose their goal and pursue it successfully and they will reign in triumph. He keeps hidden the times, the moments, the causes of all things, and when the time is right He brings forth all things from the secret treasure-chest of His wisdom, which penetrates all things irresistibly and disposes all things sweetly (Ws 8:1).

And so if anyone is brought to the point where he must either suffer torment or deny God, he need not doubt that it was God's will for him to be brought to this crisis. Therefore he has very good reason to hope for the best. For God will either extricate him from the struggle or else He will aid him in the fight and make him conquer so that He may crown him with the conqueror's wreath. "For God is trustworthy," the apostle says. "He does not allow you to be tempted beyond what you can stand, but with the temptation He also gives a way out so that you may be able to bear it" (1 Cor 10:13). Therefore, when things have come to the point of a hand-to-hand combat with the prince of this world, the devil, and his cruel underlings, and there is no way left to withdraw without disgracing the cause, then I would think that a man ought to cast away fear and I would direct him to be completely calm, confident, and hopeful. "For," says the Scripture, "whoever lacks confidence on the day of tribulation, his courage will be lessened" (Prov 24:10).

But before the actual engagement, fear is not reprehensible as long as reason does not cease to struggle against fear—a struggle which is not criminal or sinful but rather an immense opportunity for merit. For do you imagine that since those most holy martyrs shed their blood for the faith, they had no fear at all of death and torments? On this point I will not pause to draw up a list; to me Paul may stand for a thousand others. Indeed, if David was worth ten thousand soldiers in the war against the Philistines, then certainly Paul can also be considered worth ten thousand soldiers in the battle for the faith against faithless persecutors. And so this bravest of champions Paul, who was so far advanced in hope and the love of Christ that he had no doubts about his heavenly reward, who said, "I have fought the good fight, I have finished the race, and now there remains for me a crown of justice" (2 Tim 4:7–8), which he longed for so ardently that he said, "For me to live is Christ and to die is gain" and "I long to be dissolved and to be with Christ" (Phil 1:21, 23)—nevertheless this very same Paul not only managed skillfully to escape from the snares of the Jews by means of the tribune (Acts 23:6–35) but also freed himself from prison by declaring that he was a Roman citizen (Acts 22:25–29), and once again he eluded the cruelty of the Jews by appealing to Caesar (Acts 25:10–12), and he escaped the hands of the impious King Aretas by being let down from the wall in a basket (2 Cor 11:32–33).

But if anyone should contend that he was looking to the fruit that was to be planted afterwards through his efforts, and that throughout these events he was not frightened by any fear of death, certainly I will freely grant the first point, but I would not venture to assert the second. For that most brave heart of the apostle was not impervious to fear, as he himself clearly shows when he writes to the Corinthians, "For even when we came to Macedonia, our flesh had no rest but suffered all manner of affliction, conflicts without, fears within" (2 Cor 7:5). And in another place he wrote to the same persons, "I was with you in weakness and fear and much trembling" (1 Cor 2:3). And once again, "For we do not wish you, brethren, to be ignorant of the affliction which came upon us in Asia, since we were burdened beyond measure, beyond our strength, so that we were weary even of life" (2 Cor 1:8). In these passages do you not hear from Paul's own mouth his fear, his trembling, his weariness more unbearable than death itself, so that his experience seems to call to mind that agony of Christ and to present, as it were, an image of it? Go ahead now and deny if you can that Christ's holy martyrs felt fear at the terrible prospect of death. But on the other hand, no amount of terror, however great, could deter this same Paul from his program of advancing the faith, and no advice from the disciples could persuade him not to go to Jerusalem (to which he felt he was called by the Spirit of God), even though the prophet Agabus had foretold that chains and certain dangers were awaiting him there (Acts 21:10–13).

And so the fear of death and torments carries no stigma of guilt but rather is an affliction of the sort Christ came to suffer, not to escape. We should not immediately consider it cowardice for someone to feel fear and horror at the thoughts of torments, not even if he prudently avoids dangers (provided he does not compromise himself); but to flee because of a fear of torture and death when the circumstances make it necessary to fight, or to give up all hope of victory and surrender to the enemy, that, to be sure, is a capital crime according to the [Justinian] military code. But otherwise, no matter how much the heart of the soldier is agitated and stricken by fear, if he still comes forward at the command of the general, goes on, fights, and defeats the enemy, he has no reason to fear that his former fear might lessen his reward in any way. As a matter of fact, he ought to receive even more praise because of it, since he had to overcome not only the enemy but also his own fear, which is often harder to conquer than the enemy himself.

As for our Savior Christ, what happened a little after showed how far He was from letting His sadness, fear, and weariness prevent Him from obeying His Father's command and keep Him from carrying out with courage all those things which He had formerly regarded with a wise and wholesome fear. For the time being, however, He had more than one reason why He should choose to suffer fear, sadness, weariness, and grief—"chose," I say, not "be forced," for who could have forced God? Quite the contrary, it was by His own marvelous arrangement that His divinity moderated its influence on His humanity for such a time and in such a way that He was able to yield to the passion of our frail humanity and to suffer them with such terrible intensity. But as I was saying, Christ, in His wonderful generosity, chose to do this for a number of reasons.

First of all, in order to do that for which He came into the world—that is, to bear witness to the truth. And then, although He was truly man and also truly God, still there have been some who, seeing the truth of His human nature in His hunger, thirst, sleep, weariness, and suchlike, have falsely persuaded themselves that He was not true God—I do not mean the Jews and gentiles of His time who rejected Him, but rather the people of a much later time who even professed His name and His faith, namely, heretics like Arius and his followers, who denied that Christ was of one nature with the Father and thus embroiled the Church in great strife for many years. But against such plagues as this Christ provided a very powerful antidote, the endless supply of His miracles.

But there also arose an equal danger on the other side, just as those who escaped Scylla had to cope with Charybdis. For there were some who fixed their gaze so intently on the glory of His signs and powers that they were stunned and dazed by that immense brightness and went so far wrong as to deny altogether that He was truly a man. These people too, growing from their original founder into a sect, did not hesitate to rend the holy unity of the Catholic Church and to tear it apart with their disgraceful sedition. This insane belief of theirs, which is no less dangerous than it is false, seeks to undermine and subvert completely (so far as lies within their power) the mystery of mankind's redemption, since it strives to utterly cut off and dry up the spring (as it were) from which the stream of our salvation flowed forth, namely, the death and passion of our Savior. And so, to cure this very deadly disease, the best and kindest of physicians chose to experience sadness, dread, weariness, and fear of tortures and thus to show by these very real signs of human frailty that He was really a man.

Moreover, because He came into the world to earn joy for us by His own sorrow, and since that future joy of ours was to be fulfilled in our souls as well as our bodies, so too He chose to experience not only the pain of torture in His body but also the most bitter feelings of sadness, fear, and weariness in His mind, partly in order to bind us to Him all the more by reason of His greater sufferings for us, partly in order to admonish us how wrong it is for us either to refuse to suffer grief for His sake (since He freely bore so many and such immense griefs for us) or to tolerate grudgingly the punishment due to our sins, since we see our holy Savior Himself endured by His own free choice such numerous and bitter kinds of torment, both bodily and mental—and that not because He deserved them through any fault of His own, but rather in order to do away with the wicked deeds which we alone committed.

Finally, since nothing was hidden from His eternal foreknowledge, He foresaw that there would be people of various temperaments in the Church (which is His own mystical body)—that His members (I say) would differ considerably in their makeup. And although nature alone, without the help of grace, is quite incapable of enduring martyrdom (since, as the apostle says, "no one can say 'Jesus is Lord' except in the Spirit" [1 Cor 12:3]), nevertheless God does not impart grace to men in such a way as to suspend for the moment the functions and duties of nature, but instead He either allows nature to accommodate itself to the grace which is superadded to it, so that the good deed may be performed with all the more ease, or else, if nature is disposed to resist, so that this very resistance, overcome and put down by grace, may add to the merit of the deed because it was difficult to do.

Therefore, since He foresaw that there would be many people of such a delicate constitution that they would be convulsed with terror at any danger of being tortured, He chose to enhearten them by the example of His own sorrow, His own sadness, His own weariness and unequalled fear, lest they should be so disheartened as they compare their own fearful state of mind with the boldness of the bravest martyrs that they would yield freely what they fear will be won from them by force. To such a person as this, Christ wanted His own deed to speak out (as it were) with His own living voice: "O faint of heart, take courage and do not despair. You are afraid, you are sad, you are stricken with weariness and dread of the torment with which you have been cruelly threatened. Trust me. I conquered the world, and yet I suffered immeasurably more from fear, I was sadder, more afflicted with weariness, more horrified at the prospect of such cruel suffering drawing eagerly nearer and nearer. Let the brave man have his high-spirited martyrs, let him rejoice in imitating a thousand of them. But you, my timorous and feeble little sheep, be content to have me alone as your shepherd, follow my leadership; if you do not trust yourself, place your trust in me. See, I am walking ahead of you along this fearful road. Take hold of the border of my garment and you will feel going out from it a power which will stay your heart's blood from issuing in vain fears and will make your mind more cheerful, especially when you remember that you are following closely in my footsteps (and I am to be trusted and will not allow you to be tempted beyond what you can bear, but I will give together with the temptation a way out that you may be able to endure it), and likewise when you remember that this light and momentary burden of tribulation will prepare you for a weight of glory which is beyond all measure. For the sufferings of this time are not worthy to be compared with the glory to come which will be revealed in you. As you reflect on such things, take heart and use the sign of my cross to drive away this dread, this sadness, fear and weariness like vain specters of the darkness. Advance successfully and press through all obstacles, firmly confident that I will champion your cause until you are victorious and then in turn will reward you with the laurel crown of victory."

And so among the other reasons why our Savior deigned to take upon Himself these feelings of human weakness, this one I have spoken of is not unworthy of consideration—I mean that having made Himself weak for the sake of the weak, He might take care of other weak men by means of His own weakness. He had their welfare so much at heart that this whole process of His agony seems designed for nothing more clearly than to lay down a fighting technique and battle code for the fainthearted soldier who needs to be swept along, as it were, into martyrdom.

For in order to teach anyone assailed by a fear of imminent danger that he should both ask others to watch and pray and still place his trust in God alone apart from the others, and likewise in order to signify that He would tread the bitter winepress of His cross alone without any companion (Is 63:3), He commanded those same three apostles whom He had chosen from the other eight and taken on with Him almost to the foot of the mount, to stop there and to bear up and watch with Him; but He Himself withdrew from them about a stone's throw.

Question for St. Thomas More

1. We have all seen people whose fear of death causes them to become bitter and despairing at the hour of death. Explain how fear of death does not necessarily distort or impede our dying well.

St. Thomas More, Part II

Tower of London
1534

A letter of Thomas More to his daughter Margaret Roper

The Holy Spirit of God be with you.

If I would with my writing (mine own good daughter) declare how much pleasure and comfort your daughterly loving letters were unto me, a peck of coals would not suffice to make me the pens. And other pens have I (good Margaret) none here: and therefore can I write you no long process, nor dare adventure, good daughter, to write often.

The cause of my close keeping again did of likelihood grow of my negligent and very plain true word which you remember. And verily where as my mind gave me (as I told you in the garden) that some such thing were likely to happen, so doth my mind always give me that some folk yet think that I was not so poor as it appeared in the search, and that it may therefore happen that yet eftsoon ofterthan once, some new sudden searches may hap to be made in every house of ours as narrowly as

From: *St. Thomas More: Selected Letters*, ed. Elizabeth Frances Rogers (New Haven, CT: Yale University Press, 1967), pp. 234–239. Used by permission of Yale University Press.

is possible. Which thing if ever it so should hap can make but game to us that know the truth of my poverty but if they find out my wife's gay girdle and her golden beads. Howbeit I verily believe in good faith that the King's Grace of his benign pity will take nothing from her.

I thought and yet think that it may be that I was shut up upon some new causeless suspicion, grown peradventure upon some secret sinister information, whereby some folk haply thought that there should be found out against me some other greater things. But I thank our Lord whensoever this conjecture hath fallen in my mind, the clearness of my conscience hath made my heart hop for joy. For one thing am I very sure of hitherto, and trust in God's mercy to be while I live, that as often I have said unto you, I shall for anything toward my prince never take great harm, but if I take great wrong, in the sight of God, I say, howsoever it shall seem in the sight of men. For to the world, wrong may seem right sometime by false conjecturing, sometimes by false witnesses, as that good Lord said unto you, which is I dare say my very good lord in his mind, and said it of very good will. Before the world also, my refusing of this oath is accounted an heinous offense, and my religious fear toward God is called obstinacy toward my Prince. But my Lords of the Council before whom I refused it might well perceive by the heaviness of my heart appearing well more ways than one unto them that all sturdy stubbornness whereof obstinacy groweth was very far from my mind. For the clearer proof whereof, sith they seemed to take for one argument of obstinacy in me that refusing of the oath, I would not declare the causes why, I offered with a full heart, that albeit I rather would endure all the pain and peril of the statute than by declaring of the causes, give any occasion of exasperation unto my most dread Sovereign Lord and Prince, yet rather than his Highness should for not disclosing the causes account me for stubborn and obstinate, I would upon such his gracious license and commandment as should discharge me of his displeasure and peril of any statute declare those points that prevented my poor conscience to receive that oath; and would over that be sworn before, that if I should after the causes disclosed and declared find them so answered as my conscience should think itself satisfied, I would thereupon swear the oath that I there refused. To this, Master Secretary answered me that though the King's Grace gave me such a license, yet it could not discharge me against the statutes in saying anything that were by them upon heinous pains prohibited. In this good warning he showed himself my special tender friend.

And now you see well, Margaret, that it is no obstinacy to leave the causes undeclared, while I could not declare them without peril. But now is it accounted great obstinacy that I refuse the oath, whatsoever my causes be, considering that of so many wiser and better men none scrupled thereat. And Master Secretary of a great zeal that he bare unto me sware there before them a great oath that for the displeasure that he thought the King's Highness would bear me, and the suspicion that his Grace would conceive of me, which would now think in his mind that all the Nun's business was wrought and devised by me, he had leifer than I should have refused the oath that his own only son (which is a goodly young gentleman of whom our Lord send him much joy) had had his head stricken off. This word Margaret, as it was a marvelous declaration of Master Secretary's great good mind and favor toward me, so was it an heavy hearing to me that the King's Grace, my most dread Sovereign Lord, were likely to conceive such high suspicion of me and bear such grievous indignation toward me, for the thing which without the danger and peril of my poor soul lay not in my hand to help, nor doth.

Now have I heard since that some say that this obstinate manner of mine in still refusing the oath shall peradventure force and drive the King's Grace to make a further law for me. I cannot prevent such a law to be made. But I am very sure that if I died by such a law, I should die for that point innocent afore God. And albeit (good daughter) that I think our Lord that hath the hearts of Kings in his hand would never suffer of his high goodness, so gracious a Prince, and so many honorable men, and so many good men as be in the Parliament to make such an unlawful law, as that should be if it so mishapped, yet lest I note that point unthought upon, but many times more than one revolved and cast in my mind before my coming hither, both that peril and all other that might put my body in peril of death by the refusing of this oath. In devising whereupon, albeit (mine own good daughter) that I found myself (I cry God mercy) very sensual and my flesh much more shrinking from pain and from death than methought it the part of a faithful Christian man, in such a case as my conscience gave me, that in the saving of my body should stand the loss of my soul, yet I thank our Lord, that in the conflict the Spirit had in conclusion the mastery, and reason with help of faith finally concluded that for to be put to death wrongfully for doing well (as I am very sure I do, in refusing to swear against mine own conscience, being such as I am not upon peril of my soul bounden to change whether my death should come without law, or by color of a law) it is a case in which a man may lose his head and yet have none harm, but instead of harm inestimable good at the hand of God.

And I thank our Lord (Megge) since I am come hither I esteem death every day less than other. For though a man lose of his years in this world, it is more than manifold recompensed by coming the sooner to heaven. And though it be a pain to die while a man is in health, yet see I very few that in sickness die with ease. And finally, very sure am I that whensoever the time shall come that may hap to come, God wot how soon, in which I should lie sick in my death bed by nature, I shall then think that God had done much for me, if he had suffered me to die before by the color of such a law. And therefore my reason showeth me (Margaret) that it were great folly for me to be sorry to come to that death, which I would after wish that I had died. Beside that, that a man may hap with less thank of God and more peril of his soul to die as violently and as painfully by many other chances as by enemies or thieves. And therefore mine own good daughter I assure you (thanks be to God) the thinking of any such albeit it hath grieved me ere this, yet at this day grieveth me nothing. And yet I know well for all this mine own frailty, and that Saint Peter which feared it much less than I, fell in such fear soon after that at the word of a simple girl he forsook and forswore our Savior [Mt 26:69–75]. And therefore am I not (Megge) so mad as to warrant myself to stand. But I shall pray, and I pray thee mine own good daughter to pray with me, that it may please God that hath given me this mind, to give me the grace to keep it.

And thus have I mine own good daughter disclosed unto you the very secret bottom of my mind, referring the order thereof only to the goodness of God, and that so fully that I assure you Margaret on my faith I never have prayed God to bring me hence nor deliver me from death, but referring all thing whole unto his only pleasure, as to him that seeth better what is best for me than myself doth. Nor never longed I since I came hither to set foot in mine own house, for any desire of or pleasure of my house, but gladly would I sometime somewhat talk with my friends, and specially my wife and you that pertain to my charge. But sith that God otherwise disposeth, I commit all wholly to his goodness and take daily great comfort in that I perceive that you live together so charitably and so quietly; I beseech our Lord continue it. And thus, mine own good daughter, putting you finally in remembrance that albeit if the necessity so should require, I thank our Lord in this quiet and comfort is mine heart at this day, and I trust in God's goodness so shall have grace to continue, yet (as I said before) I verily trust that God shall so inspire and govern the King's heart that he shall not suffer his noble heart and courage to requite my true faithful heart and service with such extreme unlawful and uncharitable dealing, only for the displeasure that I cannot think so as other do. But his true subject will I live and die, and truly pray for him will I, both here and in the other world too.

And thus mine own good daughter have me recommended to my good bedfellow and all my children, men, women, and all, with all your babes and your nurses and all the maids and all the servants, and all our kin, and all our other friends abroad. And I beseech our Lord to save them all and keep them. And I pray you all pray for me, and I shall pray for you all. And take no thought for me whatsoever you shall hap to hear, but be merry in God.

Questions for St. Thomas More

1. Why is St. Thomas More willing to be put to death?
2. Meditate upon his trust in God's providential will. Why does he trust even though he knows he may soon be put to death?

St. John of the Cross

A great theologian, poet, and lover of Christ, St. John of the Cross (1542–1591), a Spanish Carmelite, participated with St. Teresa in the reform of the Order. In order to express his mystical experiences of Christ's presence, he composed both poetry and lengthy commentary upon his poems. The following is an excerpt from his commentary upon his *Spiritual Canticle*. His entire life depicts what he calls "[t]he soul desiring to be possessed by this immense God." Such desire in life is already a foretaste of death, which is itself an eternal embracing of the inexhaustibly glorious God.

IT SHOULD BE KNOWN that the loving Bridegroom of souls cannot long watch them suffering alone—as this soul is suffering—because, as he says through Zechariah, their afflictions touch him in the apple of his eye [Zech. 2:8], especially when these afflictions are the outcome of love for him, as are those of this soul. He also declares through Isaiah: *Before they call, I will hear; while they are yet with the word in their mouth, I will hear them* [Is. 65:24]. The Wise Man says of him that if the soul seeks him as money, she will find him [Prv. 2:4–5].

From *The Collected Works of St. John of the Cross*, pp. 510–515, translated by Kieran Kavanaugh and Otilio Rodriguez © 1979, 1991 by Washington Province of Discalced Carmelites, ICS Publications, 2131 Lincoln Road N.E., Washington, DC 20002-1199, www.icspublications.org.

Apparently God granted a certain spiritual feeling of his presence to this loving soul whose prayers are so enkindled and who seeks him more covetously than people seek money, since she has left herself and all things for him. In this spiritual sense of his presence, he revealed some deep glimpses of his divinity and beauty by which he greatly increased her fervor and desire to see him. As a man throws water into the forge to stir up and intensify the fire, so the Lord usually grants certain signs of his excellence to some souls that walk in these fiery longings of love to make them more fervent and further prepare them for the favors he wishes to grant them later. Since the soul saw and experienced through that obscure presence the supreme good and beauty hidden there, she recites the following stanza, dying with the desire to see him: Reveal your presence, and may the vision of your beauty be my death; for the sickness of love is not cured except by your very presence and image.

The soul desiring to be possessed by this immense God, for love of whom she feels that her heart is stolen and wounded, unable to suffer her sickness any longer, deliberately asks him in this stanza to show her his beauty, his divine essence, and to kill her with this revelation and thereby free her from the flesh, since she cannot see and enjoy him as she wants. She makes this request by displaying before him the sickness and yearning of her heart, in which she perseveres in suffering for love of him, unable to find a cure in anything less than this glorious vision of his divine essence. The verse follows: Reveal your presence.

In explanation of this verse it should be known that God's presence can be of three kinds:

The first is his presence by essence. In this way he is present not only in the holiest souls but also in sinners and all other creatures. With this presence he gives them life and being. Should this essential presence be lacking to them, they would all be annihilated. Thus this presence is never wanting to the soul.

The second is his presence by grace, in which he abides in the soul, pleased and satisfied with it. Not all have this presence of God; those who fall into mortal sin lose it. The soul cannot know naturally if it has this presence.

The third is his presence by spiritual affection, for God usually grants his spiritual presence to devout souls in many ways by which he refreshes, delights, and gladdens them.

Yet these many kinds of spiritual presence, just as the others, are all hidden, for in them God does not reveal himself as he is, since the conditions of this life will not allow such a manifestation. Thus the above verse "reveal your presence" could be understood of any of these three ways in which God is present.

Since it is certain that at least in the first way God is ever present in the soul, she does not ask him to be present in her but that he so reveal his hidden presence, whether natural, spiritual, or affective, that she may be able to see him in his divine being and beauty. Since he both gives the soul natural being through his essential presence and perfects her through his presence by grace, she begs him to glorify her also with his manifest glory.

Yet insofar as this soul is full of fervor and tender love of God, we should understand that this presence she asks the Beloved to reveal refers chiefly to a certain affective presence the Beloved accords her. This presence is so sublime that the soul feels an immense hidden being from which God communicates to her some semi-clear glimpses of his divine beauty. And these bear such an effect on the soul that she ardently longs and faints with desire for what she feels hidden there in that presence. This is similar to what David felt when he exclaimed: *My soul longs and faints for the courts of the Lord* [Ps. 84:2].

At this time the soul faints with longing to be engulfed in that supreme good she feels present and hidden, for although it is hidden she has a notable experience of the good and delight present there. Accordingly she is drawn and carried toward this good more forcibly than any material object is pulled toward its center by gravity. With this longing and heartfelt desire, unable to contain herself any longer, the soul begs: Reveal your presence.

Moses had this very experience on Mount Sinai. While standing in God's presence, he was able to get such sublime and profound glimpses of the height and beauty of the hidden divinity that, unable to endure it, he asked God twice to reveal his glory: *You say that you know me by name and that I have found favor before you. If therefore I have found favor in your presence, show me your face that I may know you and find before your eyes the grace which I desire fulfilled* [Ex. 33:12–13], that is, to reach the perfect love of the glory of God. Yet the Lord answered: *You shall not be able to see my face, for no human shall see me and live* [Ex. 33:20]. This is like saying: You ask a difficult thing of me, Moses, for such is the beauty of my face and the delight derived from the sight of my being that your soul will be unable to withstand it in a life as weak as this.

The soul knows that she cannot see him in his beauty in this kind of life. She knows this either through God's answer to Moses or through her experience of what is hidden here in the presence of God. For even though he appears only vaguely, she faints. Hence she anticipates the reply that can be made to her as it was to Moses and says:

> and may the vision of your beauty be my death;

This is like saying: Since the delight arising from the sight of your being and beauty is unendurable, and since I must die in seeing you, may the vision of your beauty be my death.

It is known that there are two sights that will kill humans because of the inability of human nature to suffer their force and vigor: one is the sight of the basilisk, from which it is said a person dies immediately; the other is the vision of God. Yet the causes are very different, for the sight of one kills through a terrible poison, and the vision of the other kills by an untold health and glorious good.

The soul does nothing very outstanding by wanting to die at the vision of the beauty of God in order to enjoy him forever. Were she to have but a glimpse of the height and beauty of God, she would not only desire death in order to see him now forever, as she here desires, but she would very gladly undergo a thousand singularly bitter deaths to see him only for a moment; and having seen him, she would ask to suffer just as many more that she might see him for another moment.

To shed further light on this verse, it should be known that when the soul asks that the vision of his beauty be her death she speaks conditionally, under the supposition that she cannot see him without dying. Were she able to see him without dying, she would not ask him to slay her, for to desire death is a natural imperfection. Yet with the supposition that this corruptible human life is incompatible with the other incorruptible life of God, she says: May the vision of your beauty be my death.

St. Paul teaches this doctrine to the Corinthians, saying: *We do not wish to be unclothed, but we desire to be clothed over, so that which is mortal may be absorbed in life* [2 Cor. 5:4]. This is like saying: We do not desire to be despoiled of the flesh, but to be clothed over with glory. Yet, observing that one cannot live simultaneously in glory and in the mortal flesh, he says to the Philippians that he desires to be set free and to be with Christ [Phil. 1:23].

Yet one may question: Why did the children of Israel formerly flee God and fear to see him lest they die, as Manoah and his wife did [Jgs. 13:22], whereas this soul desires to die at the sight of God? We reply that there are two reasons for this: First, even though the children of Israel at that time died in the grace of God, they were not to see him until the coming of Christ. It was much better for them to live in the flesh, increasing their merits and enjoying their natural life than to be in limbo, without ability to merit and suffering the darkness and spiritual absence of God. As a result they considered it a wonderful gift and favor from God to live for many years.

The second reason is based on love. Since the Israelites were not so fortified in love or so close to God through love, they feared to die upon seeing him. But because now in the law of grace the soul can see God when separated from the body, the desire to live but a short while and die in order to see him is more perfect. And even if this were false, the soul loving God as intensely as this one does would not fear to die from seeing him. True love receives all things that come from the Beloved—prosperity, adversity, even chastisement—with the same evenness of soul, since they are his will. And they afford her joy and delight because, as St. John says: *Perfect charity casts out all fear* [1 Jn. 4:18].

Death cannot be bitter to the soul that loves, for in it she finds all the sweetness and delight of love. The thought of death cannot sadden her, for what she finds is that gladness accompanies this thought. Neither can the thought of death be burdensome and painful to her, for death will put an end to all her sorrows and afflictions and be the beginning of all her bliss. She thinks of death as her friend and bridegroom, and at the thought of it she rejoices as she would over the thought of her betrothal and marriage, and she longs for the day and the hour of her death more than earthly kings long for kingdoms and principalities.

The Wise Man proclaims of this kind of death: *O death, your sentence is welcome to the person who feels need* [Ecclus. 41:2]. If it is welcome to those who feel need for earthly things, even though it does not provide for these needs but rather despoils such persons of the possessions they have, how much better will its sentence be for the soul in need of love, as is this one who is crying out for more love. For death will not despoil her of the love she possessed, but rather will be the cause of love's completeness, which she desires, and the satisfaction of all her needs.

The soul is right in daring to say, "may the vision of your beauty be my death," since she knows that at the instant she sees this beauty she will be carried away by it, and absorbed in this very beauty, and transformed in this beauty, and made beautiful like this beauty itself, and enriched and provided for like this very beauty. David declares, consequently, that the death of the saints is precious in the sight of the Lord [Ps. 116:15]. This would not be true if they did not participate in God's own grandeurs, for in the sight of God nothing is precious but what he in himself is.

Accordingly, the soul does not fear death when she loves; rather she desires it. Yet sinners are always fearful of death. They foresee that death will take everything away and bring them all evils. As David says, *the death of sinners is very evil* [Ps 34:21]. And hence, as the Wise Man says, *the remembrance of it is bitter* [Ecclus. 41:1]. Since sinners love the life of this world intensely and have little love for that of the other, they have an intense fear of death. But the soul that loves God lives more in the next life than in this, for a soul lives where it loves more than where it gives life, and thus takes little account of this temporal life. She says then: May the vision of your beauty be my death.

> for the sickness of love
> is not cured
> except by your very presence and image.

The reason lovesickness has no other remedy than the presence and the image of the beloved is that, since this sickness differs from others, its medicine also differs. In other sicknesses, following sound philosophy, contraries are cured by contraries, but love is incurable except by things in accord with love.

The reason for this is that love of God is the soul's health, and the soul does not have full health until love is complete. Sickness is nothing but the lack of health, and when the soul has not even a single degree of love she is dead. But when she possesses some degrees of love of God, no matter how few, she is then alive, yet very weak and infirm because of her little love. In the measure that love increases she will be healthier, and when love is perfect she will have full health.

It should be known that love never reaches perfection until the lovers are so alike that one is transfigured in the other. And then the love is in full health. The soul experiences within herself a certain sketch of love, which is the sickness she mentions, and she desires the completion of the sketch of this image, the image of her Bridegroom, the Word, the Son of God, who, as St. Paul says, *is the splendor of his glory and the image of his substance* [Heb. 1:3]; for this is the image referred to in this verse and into which the soul desires to be transformed through love. As a result she says: For the sickness of love is not cured except by your very presence and image.

She does well to call imperfect love "sickness," for just as a sick person is too weak for work, so is the soul that is feeble in love too weak to practice heroic virtue.

It is also noteworthy that those who feel in themselves the sickness of love, a lack of love, show they have some love, because they are aware of what they lack through what they have. Those who do not feel this sickness show they either have no love or are perfect in love.

Questions for St. John of the Cross

1. Describe the kinds of God's presence in our souls.
2. What is the sickness of love, and how can it assist our dying?
3. Can we both fear death and look forward to it?

St. Francis de Sales

St. Francis de Sales (1567–1622), Bishop of Geneva, is renowned for his gifts as a master of the spiritual life. The eldest of thirteen children, he knew well the tests and trials experienced in everyday life. In his ministry he collaborated with St. Jane de Chantal, a widow with whom his young sister Jane de Sales suddenly died. The following is his letter to St. Jane de Chantal describing his family's response to this devastating event. His spirituality emphasizes that we must receive the good and the bad in our lives in a spirit of radical trust that God will work good out of everything—in other words, radical abandonment to divine Providence.

To Jane de Chantal, on the Death of Francis's Younger Sister

My dear daughter,

Ah, well, is it not reasonable that the most holy will of God should be done, as much in the things we cherish as in others? But I must hasten to tell you that my good mother has drunk this chalice with an entirely

From: Francis de Sales, *Thy Will Be Done: Letters to Persons in the World* (Manchester, NH: Sophia Institute Press, 1995) pp. 123–128. Used by permission of Sophia Institute Press.

Christian constancy, and her virtue, of which I had always a high opinion, has far exceeded my estimation.

On Sunday morning, she sent for my brother the Canon; and because she had seen him very sad, and all the other brothers as well, the night before, she began by saying to him, "I have dreamt all the night that my daughter Jane is dead. Tell me, I beseech you, is it not true?" My brother, who was awaiting my arrival to break it to her (for I was on my episcopal visitation), saw this good opening for presenting the chalice to her. "It is true, mother," he said, and no more, for he had not strength to add anything. "God's will be done," said my good mother, and wept abundantly for some space; and then, calling her maid Nicole, she said, "I want to get up and go pray to God in the chapel for my poor daughter," and immediately did what she said. Not a single word of impatience, not a look of disquiet; but the blessings of God, and a thousand resignations in her will. Never did I see a calmer grief; such tears that it was a marvel, but all from simple tenderness of heart, without any sort of passion, even though it was her own dear child. Ah! Should I not then love this mother well?

Yesterday, All Saints' Day, I was the grand confessor of the family, and with the most Holy Sacrament I scaled the heart of this mother against all sadness. For the rest, she thanks you infinitely for the care and maternal love which you have shown toward this deceased little one, with as much obligation to you as if God had preserved her by your means. My brothers say as much, who in truth have manifested extremely good dispositions in the affliction, especially our Boisy, whom I love the more for it.

I will know that you would gladly ask me, "And you, how did you bear it yourself?" Yes, for you want to know how I am doing. Ah, my child, I am as human as I can be; my heart was grieved more than I should ever have thought. But the truth is that the pain to my mother and your pain have greatly increased mine; for I have feared for your heart, and my mother's. But as for the rest, *vive Jésus*, I will always take the side of divine Providence: it does all well, and disposes all things for the best. What happiness for this dear child to have been "taken away, lest wickedness should alter her understanding," [Wis. 4:11] and to have left this miry place before she had gotten soiled therein! We gather strawberries and cherries before apples and oranges, but it is because their season requires it. Let God gather what He has planted in His orchard: He takes everything in its season.

You may think, my dear daughter, how tenderly I love this little child. I have brought her forth to her Savior, for I had baptized her with my own hand, some fourteen years ago. She was the first creature on whom I exercised my order of priesthood. I was her spiritual father, and fully promised myself one day to make out of her something good. And what made her all the more dear to me (and I speak the truth) was that she was yours.

But still, my dear child, in the midst of my heart of flesh, which has had such keen feelings about this death, I perceive deep within a certain sweetness, tranquility, and a certain gentle repose of my spirit in divine Providence, which spreads abroad in my heart a great contentment in its pains.

Here, then, are my feelings represented as far as I can. But you, what do you mean when you tell me that you found yourself on this occasion such as you were? Tell me, I beseech you: was not the needle of your compass always turning to its bright pole, to its holy star, to its God? Your heart—what has it been doing? Have you scandalized those who saw you in this matter and in this event? Now this, my dear child, tell me clearly; for, do you see, it was not right to offer either your own life or that of one of your other children in exchange for that of the departed one. No, my dear child, we must not only consent for God to strike us, but we must let it be in the place which He pleases. We must leave the choice to God, for it belongs to Him. David offered his life for that of his Absalom but it was because Absalom died reprobate [2 Sam. 18:33]. In such cases we must beseech God, but in temporal loss—O my daughter, let God touch and strike whatever string of our lute He chooses; He will never make anything but a good harmony. Lord Jesus! Without reserve, without *if*, without *but*, without exception, without limitation, Your will be done, in father, in mother, in daughter, in all and everywhere! Ah! I do not say that we must not wish and pray for their preservation; but we must not say to God, "Leave this and take that"; my dear child, we must not say so. And we will not, will we? No, no; no, my child, by help of the grace of His divine goodness.

I seem to see you, my dear child, with your vigorous heart, which loves and wills powerfully. I congratulate it thereon: for what are these half-dead hearts good for? But it behooves us to make a particular exercise, once every week, of willing and loving the will of God more vigorously, (I go further) more tenderly, more amorously, than anything in the world; and this not only in bearable occurrences, but in the most unbearable. You will find more than I can describe in the little book of the *Spiritual Combat*, which I have so often recommended to you.

Ah, my child, to speak the truth, this lesson is sublime; but so also God, for whom we learn it, is the most sublime. You have, my child, four children; you have a father-in-law, a dear brother, and then again a spiritual father: all these are very dear to you, and rightly; for God wills it. Well, now, if God took all this from you, would you not still have enough in having God? Is that not *all*, in your estimation? If we had nothing else but God, would it not be enough?

Alas! The Son of God, my dear Jesus, had scarce so much on the Cross, when, having given up and left all for love and obedience to His Father, He was as if left and given up by Him; and, as the torrent of His passion swept off His bark to desolation, hardly did He perceive the needle, which was not only turned toward, but inseparably joined with, His Father. Yes, He was one with His Father, but the inferior part knew and perceived nothing of it whatever: a trial which the divine goodness has made and will make in no other soul, for no other soul could bear it.

Well, then, my child, if God takes everything from us, He will never take Himself from us, so long as we do not will it. But more; all our losses and our separations are but for this little moment. Oh truly, for so little a time as this, we ought to have patience.

I pour myself out, it seems to me, a little too much. But why? I follow my heart, which never feels it says too much with this dear daughter. I send you the family coat of arms to satisfy you. Since it pleases you to have the funeral services where this child rests in the body, I am willing; but without great pomp, beyond what Christian custom requires: what good is the rest?

You will afterward draw out a list of all these expenses, as well as those of her illness, and send it to me, for I wish it so; and meantime we shall beseech God here for this soul, and will properly do its little honors. We shall not send for its forty days' remembrance; no, my child, so much ceremony is not becoming for a child who has no rank in this world; it would get one laughed at. You know me: I love simplicity both in life and in death. I shall be very glad to know the name and the title of the church where she is. This is all I have to say on this subject. . . .

Your very affectionate servant,

Francis

Questions for St. Francis de Sales

1. Does his abandonment to divine Providence mean that he experiences no grief?
2. Reflect on St. Francis de Sales's point that even if God took everything created away from us, this would still leave us with God—infinite riches.
3. How can Christ be the pattern for our dying?

St. Joseph Cafasso

In 1860, St. John Bosco published a short biographical sketch of his recently deceased close friend and collaborator, St. Joseph Cafasso (1811–1860). Both men were simple priests, committed to an apostolate to orphans, people condemned to death, and the poor. One could not ask for a better prayer in the face of death than that prepared by St. Joseph Cafasso and published by St. John Bosco. This prayer reflects the humility and ardent love of God that characterize the art of dying well, and of living well.

Preparation for Death

THE FOLLOWING IS THE TEXT of St. Joseph Cafasso's prayer at the foot of the cross as a preparation for death.

Great God, prostrate before Thee, I accept and adore that sentence of death which Thou hast pronounced over me. I stand awaiting the coming of my last hour and, knowing that it may come upon me at any moment, I carry myself in spirit to my deathbed to bid adieu to this world and to make now for that occasion a clear and solemn protestation of those sentiments and affections with which I intend to terminate my mortal career and enter into my eternity.

From: St. John Bosco, *St. Joseph Cafasso: Priest of the Gallows*, trans. Patrick O'Connell (Rockford, IL: Tan Books, 1983), pp. 61–67.

(1) I have sinned. I confess it with all the bitterness of my soul. I detest with my whole heart all the faults that I have committed during my life. For each of them I would be ready to die in reparation for the offence to God, and I would wish to have died a thousand times rather than have offended Him. I ask pardon of God and of men for the evil that I have done, and I will ask it until the last moment of my life in order that I may find mercy on the day of judgment.

(2) Since my wretched body has been the cause of my offending my dear God so much, with my whole heart I make a total sacrifice of it to my Lord as a just punishment for it. Not only do I resign myself to descend into the tomb, but I rejoice and thank God who has given me this means of paying my debt. Through these ashes which will remain from me in the sepulcher and by these bones which will speak for me, I will confess until the day of my resurrection that the Lord is just, and just also the sentence which has condemned me to death.

(3) I thank my parents, companions and friends for the charity they have shown me in putting up with all my defects, and I thank them for all the favors and all the assistance which in their goodness they have given me. I ask pardon of them for having given such a poor return, and for the scandal I have given them. I ask them to continue to give me the charity of their prayers, and, when I am separated from them, I firmly hope that I will see them again one day in Paradise.

(4) As God in His inscrutable Providence has wished that I should have the disposal of temporal interests, I ask pardon if I have not made the use of them that He expected of me. As He alone is Lord of all, I again place everything in His hands.

I intend that the disposition that I have made or that I shall hereafter make may be for His greater glory, and, in that portion of life that remains for me on earth, it is my firm will and determination to spend all that remains to me when my needs are satisfied, for the work of the Lord, being disposed and indeed desirous to strip myself of everything whenever God wishes it of me.

(5) With regard to the most important point, which is the spiritual preparations for that day which will be my last, I render the most sincere thanks to God for having thus disposed of me and taken me out of the world. I salute and desire and bless that day that will put an end to my own sins, and take me away from the midst of so many sins that are committed on the earth. I now in advance thank that person who will

give me the consoling message, and, until that day arrives, I shall regard it as so dear to my heart that I would not exchange it for any other day of this world.

(6) I entrust my death to the love and care of my heavenly Mother. In her tender heart I place my last hour and my last sighs. It is in the arms of this Mother that I wish to leave this world and enter my eternity. I intend that every sigh which I shall give at that moment, every breath and every look, shall be voices which call her, which solicit her help for me from Heaven, so that I may soon see her, contemplate her, embrace her and may be able to die with her help. But if, by special favor of her tender heart, she wishes to call me on a day consecrated to her, it would be a still greater consolation for me to be able to present to her the offering of my life at a time when Heaven and earth celebrate a feast in honor of her name and of her great mercies.

(7) I recommend in a special manner my passage to eternity to St. Joseph, the spouse of Mary, whose name I unworthily bear, to my guardian angel, to my two special protectors, St. Ignatius and St. Alphonsus Liguori, to all the angels and saints of Heaven, and to those souls in Paradise who remember me. I salute them all from this valley of tears, and I appeal to each one of them to pray for me that the happy day will soon come when I shall meet them face to face and enjoy with them that feast that will have no end.

(8) For everything concerned with the time and circumstances of my death, after the example of my divine Redeemer, I resign myself fully to whatever the Heavenly Father has arranged for me, and I accept the death that God in His eternal decrees considers best for me. To fulfill His will, I accept all the pains that He wishes me to suffer at the time of death. In this hardest sacrifice and in my most painful agony, I wish and intend that His holy will be always done.

(9) With my whole being I give thanks to the good God, who, by His special mercy, has willed to call me to the Faith at my birth and place me, unworthy that I am, as a son in the arms of the Church. I today renew those promises that were made for me at the sacred font. I grieve for and detest whatever there has been in my life not in conformity with those promises. I condemn and regret anything that during my life may have been wanting in obedience and respect to the Holy Roman Catholic Church. Today and always I formally declare that I wish to live in the closest communion with that good Mother. To her I entrust my ashes

that she may bless them and keep them in her custody until the day of judgment.

(10) I desire and ask for all the sacraments and comforts which our holy religion has reserved for her dying children at the hour of death; and when the Lord shall demand the sacrifice of my life, I intend to unite it to that which so many confessors of the Faith have made and to breathe forth my spirit in homage of and for the support of our holy Faith.

(11) As I am about to finish my mission on earth, I give back and consign to God that grand vocation with which He has willed to adorn me. I have no words here below to thank Him worthily for it, and I await eternity to do so. I thank with all my heart all those who have employed themselves to this end for me, and I recommend myself to each of them in order that I may obtain mercy at the great moment in which I shall be called upon to render an account of my earthly career. I shall die, and the thought consoles me that with my death there will be one less unworthy minister upon the earth, and that another more zealous and fervent priest will come to make up for my coldness and other defects.

(12) As I am certain with the certainty of faith that God can, and that He wishes, to pardon all those who repent of their sins, relying on that firm confidence which cannot be deceived, and penetrated with the most lively sorrow for my past faults, I protest that I hope most firmly for pardon of all my failings and for that attainment of my eternal salvation. Whatever be the assaults that my enemy may launch against me in life or in death, I will repeat that I believe in my God, that I hope in Him and He will save me.

(13) Now that my days are about to finish, and that time is about to vanish for me forever, I know and understand better than in the past my duty on earth, which is to know and serve my God. As long as life remains I will lament that time in which I have not loved Him, and I will repeat continually from now on, "Either to love or to die." Whatever I shall have to do or suffer in this miserable life, I intend that it be a proof of love for my God, so that living, I shall live only to love, and dying, I may die in order to love still more.

(14) The sorrow which I experience, O Lord, for not having loved Thee, the desire which I feel to love Thee ever more, renders this life burdensome and distasteful, and makes me pray Thee to shorten my days on earth, and to pardon me my Purgatory in the next life, so that I soon

may arrive at loving Thee in Paradise. I ask of Thee this grace, O Lord, not through fear of punishment—which I confess that I deserve a thousand times more—but from the sincere desire to love Thee much, to love Thee soon, and to love Thee face to face in Paradise. Let the anguish which I feel, O God, for not having loved Thee, and the danger which I am running of offending Thee and not loving Thee more, serve as my Purgatory!

(15) Finally, when I shall have departed to the grave, I desire and pray the Lord to make my memory perish on this earth so that no one shall any longer think of me except to pray for me—a favor which I ask from the charity of the faithful. I accept as penance for my sins all that shall be said against me after my death. I condemn and detest all the evil that may in the future be committed because of me. I wish that I could prevent all the sins of the world by my death, and so I would be ready to die as many times as there are sins committed on the earth. Oh! May the Lord accept this poor sacrifice so that when dying, I may have that sweetest consolation of sparing one offence to my Lord on that day.

This is my firm will and determination with which I intend to live and die in each and every moment that God may wish to dispose of me.

I place the moment of my death in the hands of my dear Mother Mary, of my good angel guardian and of my special protectors, St. Joseph, St. Ignatius and St. Alphonsus Liguori, all of whom I expect to assist me at the hour of my death and in my voyage to eternity. Amen.

Come then, welcome death. Come, but conceal thy coming, so that the hour of death may not give life back again.

It will be no longer death for thee, my soul, but a sweet sleep if, when thou art dying, Jesus assists thee, and if when thou art expiring, Mary embraces thee.

Questions for St. Joseph Cafasso

1. Describe St. Joseph Cafasso's gratitude for the gift of life. How can we attain such gratitude?
2. Describe his dependence upon God's mercy.
3. Explain why St. Joseph Cafasso does not feel that he is dying alone, but rather that his death unites him to the communion of saints.

John Henry Newman

The sermons of Blessed John Henry Newman (1801–1890) are a magnificent treasure-trove of spiritual insights. Written while he was still a relatively young man, this sermon, "The Lapse of Time," concentrates our attention upon the fact that we will die, in order to stir our minds and hearts to value every moment as an opportunity to draw closer to God, our eternal destiny. As Newman points out, the world goes on as if there were nothing but time with its worldly cares, when in fact we are on the edge of eternity, and to eternity belongs the true value. Now is the time for conversion, through faith in Christ's mercy, to the life of charity that the grace of the Holy Spirit makes possible.

The Lapse of Time

"Whatsoever thy hand findeth to do, do it with thy might; for there is no work, nor device, nor knowledge, nor wisdom, in the grave, whither thou goest."—Eccles. ix. 10.

SOLOMON'S ADVICE that we should do whatever our hand findeth to do with our might, naturally directs our thoughts to that great work in

From: John Henry Newman, *Parochial and Plain Sermons* (San Francisco: Ignatius Press, 1987), pp. 1409–1415.

which all others are included, which will outlive all other works, and for which alone we really are placed here below—the salvation of our souls. And the consideration of this great work, which must be done with all our might, and completed before the grave, whither we go, presents itself to our minds with special force at the commencement of a new year. We are now entering on a fresh stage of our life's journey; we know well how it will end, and we see where we shall stop in the evening, though we do not see the road. And we know in what our business lies while we travel, and that it is important for us to do it with our "might; for there is no work, nor device, nor knowledge, nor wisdom, in the grave." This is so plain, that nothing need be said in order to convince us that it is true. We know it well; the very complaint which numbers commonly make when told of it, is that they know it already, that it is nothing new, that they have no need to be told, and that it is tiresome to hear the same thing said over and over again, and impertinent in the person who repeats it. Yes; thus it is that sinners silence their conscience, by quarreling with those who appeal to it; they defend themselves, if it may be called a defence, by pleading that they already know what they should do and do not; that they know perfectly well that they are living at a distance from God, and are in peril of eternal ruin; that they know they are making themselves children of Satan, and denying the Lord that bought them, and want no one to tell them so. Thus they witness against themselves.

However, though we already know well enough that we have much to do before we die, yet (if we will but attend) it may be of use to hear the fact dwelt upon; because by thinking over it steadily and seriously, we may possibly, through God's grace, gain some deep conviction of it; whereas while we keep to general terms, and confess that this life is important and is short, in the mere summary way in which men commonly confess it, we have, properly speaking, no knowledge of that great truth at all.

Consider, then, what it is to die; "there is no work, device, knowledge, or wisdom, in the grave." Death puts an end absolutely and irrevocably to all our plans and works, and it is inevitable. The Psalmist speaks to "high and low, rich and poor, one with another." "No man can deliver his brother, nor make agreement unto God for him." Even "wise men die, as well as the ignorant and foolish, and leave their riches for other." Difficult as we may find it to bring it home to ourselves, to realize it, yet as surely as we are here assembled together, so surely will every one of us, sooner or later, one by one, be stretched out on the bed of death. We naturally shrink from the thought of death, and of its attendant circumstances; but all that is hateful and fearful about it will be fulfilled in our case, one by one. But all this is nothing compared with the consequences implied in it. Death stops us; it stops our race. Men are engaged about their work, or about their pleasure; they are in the city, or the field; any how they are stopped; their deeds are suddenly gathered in—a reckoning is made—all is sealed up till the great day. What a change is this! In the words used familiarly in speaking of the dead, they are no more. They were full of schemes and projects; whether in a greater or humbler rank, they had their hopes and fears, their prospects, their pursuits, their rivalries; all these are now come to an end. One builds a house, and its roof is not finished; another buys merchandise, and it is not yet sold. And all their virtues and pleasing qualities which endeared them to their friends are, as far as this world is concerned, vanished. Where are they who were so active, so sanguine, so generous? The amiable, the modest, and the kind? We were told that they were dead; they suddenly disappeared; that is all we know about it. They were silently taken from us; they are not met in the seat of the elders, nor in the assemblies of the people; in the mixed concourse of men, nor in the domestic retirement which they prized. As Scripture describes it, "the wind has passed over them, and they are gone, and their place shall know them no more." And they have burst the many ties which held them; they were parents, brothers, sisters, children, and friends; but the bond of kindred is broken, and the silver cord of love is loosed. They have been followed by the vehement grief of tears, and the long sorrow of aching hearts; but they make no return, they answer not; they do not even satisfy our wish to know that they sorrow for us as we for them. We talk about them thenceforth as if they were persons we do not know; we talk about them as third persons; whereas they used to be always with us, and every other thought which was within us was shared by them. Or perhaps, if our grief is too deep, we do not mention their names at all. And their possessions, too, all fall to others. The world goes on without them; it forgets them. Yes, so it is; the world contrives to forget that men have souls, it looks upon them all as mere parts of some great visible system. This continues to move on; to this the world ascribes a sort of life and personality. When one or other of its members die, it considers them only as falling out of the system, and as come to nought. For a minute, perhaps, it thinks of them in sorrow, then leaves them—leaves them for ever. It keeps its eye on things seen and temporal. Truly whenever a man dies, rich or poor, an immortal soul passes to judgment; but somehow we read of the deaths of persons we have seen or heard of, and this reflection never comes across us. Thus does the world really cast off men's souls, and recognizing only their bodies, it makes it appear as if "that which befalleth the sons of men befalleth beasts, even one thing befalleth them, as the one dieth so dieth the other; yea, they have all one breath, so that a man hath no pre-eminence over a beast, for all is vanity."

But let us follow the course of a soul thus casting off the world, and cast off by it. It goes forth as a stranger on a journey. Man seems to die and to be no more, when he is but quitting us, and is really beginning to live. Then he sees sights which before it did not even enter into his mind to conceive, and the world is even less to him than he to the world. Just now he was lying on the bed of sickness, but in that moment of death what an awful change has come over him! What a crisis for him! There is stillness in the room that lately held him; nothing is doing there, for he is gone, he now belongs to others; he now belongs entirely to the Lord who bought him; to Him he returns; but whether to be lodged safely in His place of hope, or to be imprisoned against the great Day, that is another matter, that depends on the deeds done in the body, whether good or evil. And now what are his thoughts? How infinitely important now appears the value of time, now when it is nothing to him! Nothing; for though he spend centuries waiting for Christ, he cannot now alter his state from bad to good, or from good to bad. What he dieth that he must be for ever; as the tree falleth so must it lie. This is the comfort of the true servant of God, and the misery of the transgressor. His lot is cast once and for all, and he can but wait in hope or in dread. Men on their death-beds have declared, that no one could form a right idea of the value of time till he came to die; but if this has truth in it, how much more truly can it be said after death! What an estimate shall we form of time while we are waiting for judgment! Yes, it is we—all this, I repeat, belongs to us most intimately. It is not to be looked at as a picture, as a man might read a light book in a leisure hour. *We* must die, the youngest, the healthiest, the most thoughtless; *we* must be thus unnaturally torn in two, soul from body; and only united again to be made more thoroughly happy or to be miserable for ever.

Such is death considered in its inevitable necessity, and its unspeakable importance—nor can we ensure to ourselves any certain interval before its coming. The time may be long! but it may also be short. It is plain, a man may die any day; all we can say is, that it is unlikely that he will die. But of this, at least, we are certain, that, come it sooner or later, death is continually on the move towards us. We are ever nearer and nearer to it. Every morning we rise we are nearer that grave in which there is no work, nor device, than we were. We are now nearer the grave, than when we entered this Church. Thus life is ever crumbling away under us. What should we say to a man, who was placed on some precipitous ground, which was ever crumbling under his feet, and affording less and less secure footing, yet was careless about it? Or what should we say to one who suffered some precious liquor to run from its receptacle into the thoroughfare of men, without a thought to stop it? who carelessly looked on and saw the waste of it, becoming greater and greater every minute? But what treasure can equal time? It is the seed of eternity: yet we suffer ourselves to go on, year after year, hardly using it at all in God's service, or thinking it enough to give Him at most a tithe or a seventh of it, while we strenuously and heartily sow to the flesh, that from the flesh we may reap corruption. We try how little we can safely give to religion, instead of having the grace to give abundantly. "Rivers of water run down mine eyes, because men keep not Thy law;" so say the holy Psalmist. Doubtless an inspired prophet saw far more clearly than we can see, the madness of men in squandering that treasure upon sin, which is meant to buy their chief good;—but if so, what must this madness appear in God's sight! What an inveterate malignant evil is it in the hearts of the sons of men, that thus leads them to sit down to eat, and drink, and rise up to play, when time is hurrying on and judgment coming? We have been told what He thinks of man's unbelief, though we cannot enter into the depths of His thoughts. He showed it to us in act and deed, as far as we could receive it, when He even sent His only-begotten Son into the world as at this time, to redeem us from the world,—which, most surely, was not lightly done; and we also learn His thoughts about it from the words of that most merciful Son,—which most surely were not lightly spoken, "The wicked," He says, "shall go into everlasting punishment."

Oh that there were such a heart in us that we would fear God and keep His commandments always! But it is of no use to speak; men know their duty—they will not do it. They say they do not need or wish to be told it, that it is an intrusion, and a rudeness, to tell them of death and judgment. So must it be,—and we, who have to speak to them, must submit to this. Speak we must, as an act of duty to God, whether they will hear, or not, and then must leave our words as a witness. Other means for rousing them we have none. We speak from Christ our gracious Lord, their Redeemer, who has already pardoned them freely, yet they will not follow Him with a true heart; and what can be done more?

Another year is now opening upon us; it speaks to the thoughtful, and is heard by those, who have expectant ears, and watch for Christ's coming. The former year is gone, it is dead, there it lies in the grave of past time, not to decay however, and be forgotten, but kept in the view of God's omniscience, with all its sins and errors irrevocably written, till, at length, it will be raised again to testify about us at the last day; and who among us can bear the thought of his own doings, in the course of it?—all that he has said and done, all that has been conceived within his mind, or been acted on, and all that he has not said and done, which it was a duty to say or do. What a dreary prospect seems to be before us, when we reflect that we have the solemn word of truth pledged to us, in the last and most awful revelation, which God has made to us about the future, that in that day, the books will be opened, "and another book opened, which is the book of life, and the dead judged out of those things which were written in the books according to their works!" What would a man give, any one of us, who has any real insight into his polluted and miserable state, what would he give to tear away some of the leaves there preserved! For how heinous are the sins therein written! Think of the multitude of sins done by us since we first knew the difference between right and wrong. We have forgotten them, but there we might read them clearly recorded. Well may holy David exclaim, "Remember not the sins of my youth nor my transgressions, according to Thy mercy remember Thou me." Conceive, too, the multitude of sins which we have so grown into us as to become part of us, and in which we now live, not knowing, or but partially knowing, that they are sins; habits of pride, self-reliance, self-conceit, sullenness, impurity, sloth, selfishness, worldliness. The history of all these, their beginnings, and their growth, is recorded in those dreadful books; and when we look forward to the future, how many sins shall we have committed by this time next year,—though we try ever so much to know our duty, and overcome ourselves! Nay, or rather shall we have the opportunity of obeying or disobeying God for a year longer? Who knows whether by that time our account may not be closed for ever?

"Remember me, O Lord, when Thou comest into Thy kingdom." Such was the prayer of the penitent thief on the cross, such must be our prayer. Who can do us any good, but He, who shall also be our Judge? When shocking thoughts about ourselves come across us and afflict us, "Remember me," this is all we have to say. We have "no work, nor device, nor knowledge, not wisdom" of our own, to better ourselves withal. We can say nothing to God in defence of ourselves,—we can but acknowledge that we are grievous sinners, and addressing Him as suppliants, merely beg Him to bear us in mind in mercy, for His Son's sake to do us some favour, not according to our deserts, but for the love of Christ. The more we try to serve Him here, the better; but after all, so far do we fall short of what we should be, that if we had but what we are in ourselves to rely upon, wretched are we,—and we are forced out of ourselves by the very necessity of our condition. To whom should we go? Who can do us any good, but He who was born into this world for our regeneration, was bruised for our iniquities, and rose again for our justification? Even though we have served Him from our youth up, though after His pattern we have grown, as far as mere man can grow, in wisdom as we grew in stature, though we ever have had tender hearts, and a mortified will, and a conscientious temper, and an obedient spirit; yet, at the very best, now much have we left undone, how much done, which ought to be otherwise! What He can do for our nature, in the way of sanctifying it, we know indeed in a measure; we know, in the case of His saints; and we certainly do not know the limit of His carrying forward in those objects of His special favour the work of purification, and renewal through His Spirit. But for ourselves, we know full well that much as we may have attempted, we have done very little, that our very best service is nothing worth,—and the more we attempt, the more clearly we shall see how little we have hitherto attempted.

Those whom Christ saves are they who at once attempt to save themselves, yet despair of saving themselves; who aim to do all, and confess they do nought; who are all love, and all fear; who are the most holy, and yet confess themselves the most sinful; who ever seek to please Him, yet feel they never can; who are full of good works, yet of works of penance. All this seems a contradiction to the natural man, but it is not so to those whom Christ enlightens. They understand in proportion to their illumination, that it is possible to work out their salvation, yet to have it wrought out for them, to fear and tremble at the thought of judgment, yet to rejoice always in the Lord, and hope and pray for His coming.

Questions for Blessed John Henry Newman

1. Can we imagine living without our "schemes and projects"? Have we grasped how transitory life is?
2. As sinners, how can we bear to die and face the holy God? How can we address our fear of being called to account for what we have done to others?
3. Why should we meditate upon death?

St. Therese of Lisieux

Perhaps the greatest saint of modern times, St. Therese of Lisieux (1873–1897) taught the "little way" of spiritual perfection—becoming holy in the little things, the small sacrifices, of everyday life. Her short life bore fruit in writings of extraordinary spiritual maturity, as she experienced the depths of child-like relationship to, and dependence upon, Jesus Christ, the living Lord. Here she describes her experiences as she approaches her death. In simple love, the greatest possible vocation is found.

O JESUS, MY BELOVED, who could express the tenderness and sweetness with which You are guiding my soul! It pleases You to cause the rays of Your grace to shine through even in the midst of the darkest storm! Jesus, the storm was raging very strongly in my soul ever since the beautiful feast of Your victory, the radiant feast of Easter; one Saturday in the month of May, thinking of the mysterious dreams which are granted at times to certain souls, I said of myself that these dreams must be a very sweet consolation, and yet I wasn't asking for such a consolation. In the evening, considering the clouds which were covering her heaven, my little soul said again within herself that these beautiful dreams were not for her.

From *Story of a Soul: The Autobiography of Saint Therese of Lisieux*, pp. 190–200, translated by John Clarke © 1996 by Washington Province of Discalced Carmelites, ICS Publications, 2131 Lincoln Road N.E., Washington, DC 20002-1199, www.icspublications.org.

And then she fell asleep in the midst of the storm. The next day was May 10, the second SUNDAY of Mary's month, and perhaps the anniversary of the day when the Blessed Virgin deigned to smile upon her little flower.

At the first glimmerings of dawn I was (in a dream) in a kind of gallery and there were several other persons, but they were at a distance. Our Mother was alone near me. Suddenly, without seeing how they had entered, I saw three Carmelites dressed in their mantles and long veils. It appeared to me they were coming for our Mother, but what I did understand clearly was that they came from heaven. In the depths of my heart I cried out: "Oh! how happy I would be if I could see the face of one of these Carmelites!" Then, as though my prayer were heard by her, the tallest of the saints advanced toward me; immediately I fell to my knees! Oh! what happiness! The Carmelite *raised her veil or rather she raised it and covered me with it.* Without the least hesitation, I recognized *Venerable Anne of Jesus*, Foundress of Carmel in France. Her face was beautiful, but with an immaterial beauty. No ray escaped from it and still, in spite of the veil which covered us both, I saw this heavenly face suffused with an unspeakably gentle light, a light it didn't receive from without but was produced from within.

I cannot express the joy of my soul since these things are experienced but cannot be put into words. Several months have passed since this sweet dream, and yet the memory it has left in my soul has lost nothing of its freshness and heavenly charms. I still see Venerable Mother's glance and smile which was FILLED with LOVE. I believe I can still feel the caresses she gave me at this time.

Seeing myself so tenderly loved, I dared to pronounce these words: "O Mother! I beg you, tell me whether God will leave me for a long time on this earth. Will he come soon to get me?" Smiling tenderly, the saint whispered: "*Yes, soon, soon, I promise you.*" I added: "Mother, tell me further if God is not asking something more of me than my poor little actions and desires. Is He content with me?" The saint's face took on an expression *incomparably more tender* than the first time she spoke to me. Her look and her caresses were the sweetest of answers. However, she said to me: "God asks no other thing from you. He is content, very content!" After again embracing me with more love than the tenderest of mothers has ever given to her child, I saw her leave. My heart was filled with joy, and then I remembered my Sisters, and I wanted to ask her some favors for them, but alas, I awoke!

O Jesus, the storm was no longer raging, heaven was calm and serene. I *believed*, I *felt* there was a *heaven* and that this *heaven* is peopled with souls who actually love me, who consider me their child. This impression remains in my heart, and this all the more because I was, up until then, *absolutely indifferent to Venerable Mother Anne of Jesus*. I never invoked her in prayer and thought of her never came to my mind except when I heard others speak of her, which was seldom. And when I understood to what a degree *she loved me*, how *indifferent* I had been toward her, my heart was filled with love and gratitude, not only for the Saint who had visited me, but for all the blessed inhabitants of heaven.

O my Beloved! this grace was only the prelude to the greatest graces You wished to bestow upon me. Allow me, my only Love, to recall them to You *today* which is the sixth anniversary of *our union*. Ah! my Jesus, pardon me if I am unreasonable in wishing to express my desires and longings which reach even unto infinity. Pardon me and heal my soul by giving her what she longs for so much!

To be Your *Spouse*, to be a *Carmelite*, and by my union with You to be the *Mother* of souls, should this not suffice me? And yet it is not so. No doubt, these three privileges sum up my true *vocation*: *Carmelite, Spouse, Mother*, and yet I feel within me other *vocations*. I feel the *vocation* of the WARRIOR, THE PRIEST, THE APOSTLE, THE DOCTOR, THE MARTYR. Finally, I feel the need and the desire for carrying out the most heroic deeds for *You, O Jesus*. I feel within my soul the courage of the *Crusader*, the *Papal Guard*, and I would want to die on the field of battle in defense of the Church.

I feel in myself the *vocation of* the PRIEST. With what love, O Jesus, I would carry You in my hands when, at my voice, You would come down from heaven. And with what love would I give You to souls! But alas! while desiring to be a *Priest*, I admire and envy the humility of St. Francis of Assisi and I feel the *vocation* of imitating him in refusing the sublime dignity of the *Priesthood*.

O Jesus, my Love, my Life, how can I combine these contrasts? How can I realize the desires of my poor *little soul*?

Ah! in spite of my littleness, I would like to enlighten souls as did the *Prophets* and the *Doctors*. I have the *vocation of the Apostle*. I would like to travel over the whole earth to preach Your Name and to plant Your glorious Cross on infidel soil. But *O my Beloved*, one mission alone would not be sufficient for me, I would want to preach the Gospel on all the five continents simultaneously and even to the most remote isles. I would be a missionary, not for a few years only, but from the beginning of creation until the consummation of the ages. But above all, O my Beloved Savior, I would shed my blood for You even to the very last drop.

Martyrdom was the dream of my youth and this dream has grown with me within Carmel's cloisters. But here again, I feel that my dream is a folly, for I cannot confine myself to desiring *one kind* of martyrdom. To satisfy me I need *all.* Like You, my Adorable Spouse, I would be scourged and crucified. I would die flayed like St. Bartholomew. I would be plunged into boiling oil like St. John; I would undergo all the tortures inflicted upon the martyrs. With St. Agnes and St. Cecilia, I would present my neck to the sword, and like Joan of Arc, my dear sister, I would whisper at the stake Your Name, O JESUS. When thinking of the torments which will be the lot of Christians at the time of Anti-Christ, I feel my heart leap with joy and I would that these torments be reserved for me. Jesus, Jesus, if I wanted to write all my desires, I would have to borrow Your *Book of Life,* for in it are reported all the actions of all the saints, and I would accomplish all of them for You.

O my Jesus! what is your answer to all my follies? Is there a soul more *little,* more powerless than mine? Nevertheless even because of my weakness, it has pleased You, O Lord, to grant my *little childish desires* and You desire, today, to grant other desires that are *greater* than the universe.

During my meditation, my desires caused me a veritable martyrdom, and I opened the Epistles of St. Paul to find some kind of answer. Chapters 12 and 13 of the First Epistle to the Corinthians fell under my eyes. I read there, in the first of these chapters, that *all* cannot be apostles, prophets, doctors, etc., that the Church is composed of different members, and that the eye cannot be the hand at *one and the same time.* The answer was clear, but it did not fulfill my desires and gave me no peace. But just as Mary Magdalene found what she was seeking by always stooping down and looking into the empty tomb, so I, abasing myself to the very depths of my nothingness, raised myself so high that I was able to attain my end. Without becoming discouraged, I continued my reading, and this sentence consoled me: "*Yet strive after* THE BETTER GIFTS, *and I point out to you a yet more excellent way.*" And the Apostle explains how all *the most* PERFECT *gifts* are nothing without LOVE. *That Charity is the* EXCELLENT WAY *that leads most surely* to God.

I finally had rest. Considering the mystical body of the Church, I had not recognized myself in any of the members described by St. Paul, or rather I desired to see myself in them *all*. *Charity* gave me the key to my *vocation*. I understood that if the Church had a body composed of different members, the most necessary and most noble of all could not be lacking to it, and so I understood that the Church *had a Heart and that this Heart* was BURNING WITH LOVE. *I understood it was Love alone* that made the Church's members act, that if *Love* ever became extinct, apostles would not preach the Gospel and martyrs would not shed their blood. I understood that LOVE COMPRISED ALL VOCATIONS, THAT LOVE WAS EVERYTHING, THAT IT EMBRACED ALL TIMES AND PLACES. . . . IN A WORD, THAT IT WAS ETERNAL!

Then, in the excess of my delirious joy, I cried out: O Jesus, my Love. . . . my *vocation*, at last I have found it. . . . MY VOCATION IS LOVE!

Yes, I have found my place in the Church and it is You, O my God, who have given me this place; in the heart of the Church, my Mother, I shall be *Love*. Thus I shall be everything, and thus my dream will be realized.

Why speak of a delirious joy? No, this expression is not exact, for it was rather the calm and serene peace of the navigator perceiving the beacon which must lead him to the port. . . . O luminous Beacon of love, I know how to reach You, I have found the secret of possessing Your flame.

I am only a child, powerless and weak, and yet it is my weakness that gives me the boldness of offering myself as VICTIM *of Your Love, O Jesus!* In times past, victims, pure and spotless, were the only ones accepted by the Strong and Powerful God. To satisfy Divine *Justice*, perfect victims were necessary, but the *law of Love* has succeeded to the law of fear, and *Love* has chosen me as a holocaust, me, a weak and imperfect creature. Is not this choice worthy of Love? Yes, in order that Love may be fully satisfied, it is necessary that It lower Itself, and that It lower Itself to nothingness and transform this nothingness into *fire*.

O Jesus, I know it, love is repaid by love alone, and so I searched and I found the way to solace my heart by giving you Love for Love. "Make use of the riches which render one unjust in order to make friends who will receive you into everlasting dwellings." Behold, Lord, the counsel You give Your disciples after having told them that "The children of this world, in relation to their own generation, are more prudent than are the children of the light." A child of light, I understood that my *desires of being everything*, of embracing all vocations, were the riches that would be able to render me unjust, so I made use of them *to make friends*. Remembering the prayer of Elisha to his Father Elijah when he dared to ask him for HIS DOUBLE SPIRIT, I presented myself before the angels and saints and I said to them: "I am the smallest of creatures; I know my misery and my feebleness, but I know also how much noble and generous hearts love to do good. I beg you then, O Blessed Inhabitants of heaven, I beg you to ADOPT ME AS YOUR CHILD. *To you alone will be the glory* which you will make me merit, but deign to answer my prayer. It is bold, I know; however, I dare ask you to obtain for my YOUR TWOFOLD LOVE."

Jesus, I cannot fathom the depths of my request; I would be afraid to find myself overwhelmed under the weight of my bold desires. My excuse is that I am a *child*, and children do not reflect on the meaning of their words; however, their parents, once they are placed upon a throne and possess immense treasures, do not hesitate to satisfy the desires of the *little ones* whom they love as much as they love themselves. To please them they do foolish things, even going to the extent of *becoming weak* for them. Well, I am the *Child of the Church* and the Church is a Queen since she is Your Spouse, O divine King of kings. The heart of a child does not seek riches and glory (even the glory of heaven). She understands that this glory belongs by right to her brothers, the angels and saints. Her own glory will be the reflected glory which shines on her Mother's forehead. What this child asks for is Love. She knows only one thing: to love You, O Jesus. Astounding works are forbidden to her; she cannot preach the Gospel, shed her blood; but what does it matter since her brothers work in her stead and she, *a little child*, stays very close to the *throne* of the King and Queen. She loves in her brothers' place while they do the fighting. But how will she prove her *love* since *love* is proved by works? Well, the little child *will strew flowers*, she will perfume the royal throne with their sweet scents, and she will sing in her silvery tones the canticle of *Love*.

Yes, my Beloved, this is how my life will be consumed. I have no other means of proving my love for you other than that of strewing flowers, that is, not allowing one little sacrifice to escape, not one look, one word, profiting by all the smallest things and doing them through love. I desire to suffer for love and even to rejoice through love; and in this way I shall strew flowers before Your throne. I shall not come upon one without *unpetalling* it for You. While I am strewing my flowers, I shall sing, for could one cry while doing such a joyous action? I shall sing even when I must gather my flowers in the midst of thorns, and my song will be all the more melodious in proportion to the length and sharpness of the thorns.

O Jesus, of what use will my flowers be to You? Ah! I know very well that this fragrant shower, these fragile, worthless petals, these songs of love from the littlest of hearts will charm You. Yes, these nothings will please You. They will bring a smile to the Church Triumphant. She will gather up my flowers unpetalled *through love* and have them pass through Your own divine hands, O Jesus. And this Church in heaven, desirous of playing with her little child, will cast these flowers, which are now infinitely valuable because of Your divine touch, upon the Church Suffering in order to extinguish its flames and upon the Church Militant in order to gain the victory for it!

O my Jesus! I love You! I love the Church, my Mother! I recall that *"the smallest act of PURE LOVE is of more value to her than all other works together."* But is PURE LOVE in my heart? Are my measureless desires only but a dream, a folly? Ah! if this be so, Jesus, then enlighten me, for You know I am seeking only the truth. If my desires are rash, then make them disappear, for these desires are the greatest martyrdom to me. However, I feel, O Jesus, that after having aspired to the most lofty heights of Love, if one day I am not to attain them, I feel that I shall have tasted *more sweetness in my martyrdom and my folly* than I shall taste in the bosom of the *joy of the Fatherland*, unless you take away the memory of these earthly hopes through a miracle. Allow me to taste the sweet bitterness of my martyrdom.

Jesus, O Jesus, if the *desire of loving You* is so delightful, what will it be to possess and enjoy this Love?

How can a soul as imperfect as mine aspire to the possession of the plenitude of *Love*? O Jesus, *my first and only Friend*, You whom *I love* UNIQUELY, explain this mystery to me! Why do you not reserve these aspirations for great souls, for the *Eagles* that soar in the heights?

I look upon myself as a *weak little bird*, with only a light down as covering. I am not an *eagle*, but I have only an eagle's EYES AND HEART. In spite of my extreme littleness I still dare to gaze upon the Divine Sun, the Sun of Love, and my heart feels within it all the aspirations of an *Eagle*.

The little bird wills *to fly* toward the bright Sun that attracts its eye, imitating its brothers, the eagles, whom it sees climbing up toward the Divine Furnace of the Holy Trinity. But alas! the only thing it can do is *raise its little wings*; to fly is not within its *little* power!

What then will become of it? Will it die of sorrow at seeing itself so weak? Oh no! the little bird will not even be troubled. With bold surrender, it wishes to remain gazing upon its Divine Sun. Nothing will frighten it, neither wind nor rain, and if dark cloud come and hide the Star of Love, the little bird will not change its place because it knows that beyond the clouds its bright Sun still shines on and that its brightness is not eclipsed for a single instant.

At times the little bird's heart is assailed by the storm, and it seems it should believe in the existence of no other thing except the clouds surrounding it; this is the moment of perfect joy for the poor weak little creature. And what joy it experiences when remaining there just the same! and gazing at the Invisible Light which remains hidden from its faith!

O Jesus, up until the present moment I can understand Your love for the little bird because it has not strayed far from You. But I know and so do You that very often the imperfect little creature, while remaining in its place (that is, under the Sun's rays), allows itself to be somewhat distracted from its sole occupation. It picks up a piece of grain on the right or on the left; it chases after a little worm; then coming upon a little pool of water, it wets its feathers still hardly formed. It sees an attractive flower and its little mind is occupied with this flower. In a word, being unable to soar like the eagles, the poor little bird is taken up with the trifles of earth.

And yet after all these misdeeds, instead of going and hiding away in a corner to weep over its misery and to die of sorrow, the little bird turns toward its beloved Sun, presenting its wet wings to its beneficent rays. It cries like a swallow and in its sweet song it recounts in detail all its infidelities, thinking in the boldness of its full trust it will acquire in even greater fullness the love of *Him* who came to call not the just but sinners. And even if the Adorable Star remains deaf to the plaintive chirping of the little creature, even if it remains hidden, well, the little one will remain *wet*, accepting its numbness from the cold and rejoicing in its suffering which it knows it deserves.

O Jesus, Your *little bird* is happy to be *weak and little*. What would become of it if it were big? Never would it have the boldness to appear in

Your presence, to *fall asleep* in front of You. Yes, this is still one of the weaknesses of the little bird: when it wants to fix its gaze upon the Divine Sun, and when the clouds prevent it from seeing a single ray of that Sun, in spite of itself, its little eyes close, its little head is hidden beneath its wing, and the poor little thing falls asleep, believing all the time that it is fixing its gaze upon its Dear Star. When it awakens, it doesn't feel desolate; its little heart is at peace and it begins once again its work of *love*. It calls upon the angels and the saints who rise like eagles before the consuming Fire, and since this is the object of the little bird's desire the eagles take pity on it, protecting and defending it, and putting to flight at the same time the vultures who want to devour it. These vultures are the demons whom the little bird doesn't fear, for it is not destined to be their *prey* but the prey of the *Eagle* whom it contemplates in the center of the Sun of Love.

O Divine Word! You are the Adored Eagle whom I love and who alone *attracts me*! Coming into this land of exile, You willed to suffer and to die in order *to draw* souls to the bosom of the Eternal Fire of the Blessed Trinity. Ascending once again to the Inaccessible Light, henceforth Your abode, You remain still in this "valley of tears," hidden beneath the appearances of a white host. Eternal Eagle, You desire to nourish me with Your divine substance and yet I am but a poor little thing who would return to nothingness if Your divine glance did not give me life from one moment to the next.

O Jesus, allow me in my boundless gratitude to say to You that Your love *reaches unto folly*. In the presence of this folly, how can You not desire that my heart leap toward You? How can my confidence, then, have any limits? Ah! the saints have committed their *follies* for You, and they have done great things because they are eagles.

Jesus, I am too little to perform great actions, and my own *folly* is this: to trust that Your Love will accept me as a victim. My *folly* consists in begging the eagles, my brothers, to obtain for me the favor of flying toward the Sun of Love with the *Divine Eagle's own wings!*

As long as You desire it, O my Beloved, Your little bird will remain without strength and without wings and will always stay with its gaze fixed upon You. It wants to be *fascinated* by Your divine glance. It wants to become the *prey* of Your Love. One day I hope that You, the Adorable Eagle, will come to fetch me, Your little bird; and ascending with it to the Furnace of Love, You will plunge if for all eternity into the burning Abyss of this Love to which it has offered itself as victim.

O Jesus! why can't I tell all *little souls* how unspeakable is Your condescension? I feel that if You found a soul weaker and littler than mine, which is impossible, You would be pleased to grant it still greater favors, provided it abandoned itself with total confidence to Your Infinite Mercy. But why do I desire to communicate Your secrets of Love, O Jesus, for was it not You alone who taught them to me, and can You not reveal them to others? Yes, I know it, I and beg You to do it. I beg You to cast Your Divine glance upon a great number of *little* souls. I beg You to choose a legion of *little* Victims worthy of Your LOVE!

Questions for St. Therese of Lisieux

1. Describe St. Therese's dream.
2. As she lays dying, how does she address her desire to accomplish all sorts of goals in this world?
3. In admitting that we have no strength of our own, we enter into the mystery of divine love. Why is this so?

Index

Absalom, 105
Adeodatus, 47
Alexander, 23
Ambrose, St., xviii, 33–42, 48
Anne of Jesus, 124–25
Anthony, St., xviii, 27–31; death of, 28–30
Arians, 30, 85
Athanasius, St., xvi, xviii, 27, 30
Attalus, 18, 21–23
Augustine, St., xviii, 33, 43–51, 54, 56, 58, 60
autonomy, xiv

baptism, 54, 105
Biblias, 19
Blandina, 18, 21, 23–24
Brave New World, xi
Brothers Karamazov, The, xvi
burial, 46, 48, 106

Cafasso, Joseph, St., xix, 109–13
Carmelite Order, 95, 124–25
Catherine of Genoa, St., xviii, 73–78
Catherine of Siena, St., xviii, 65–71

charity, 57, 58, 67–69, 75–76, 100–1, 105, 109, 112, 125–32
Church, Catholic, 7, 10, 22, 51, 86, 111, 128–29; as mystical body, 127; in Rome, 1; in Smyrna, 13; in Syria, 4
common good, 62–63
communion of saints, 125
confession, sacrament of, 104
confirmation, sacrament of, 20
consolation, 39, 41, 123–24
conversion, 115
1 Corinthians, xv, 126
cruciformity, xx
Cyprian, 56

damnation, 65, 119
David, King, 105, 120
darkness, mystical, xv, xix, 130
death, xv, xix, 116–19; desire for, 70, 75, 96–101, 112; fear of, xvi, 81, 84, 91, 100; for Christ's sake, 60; preparation for, xix, 109–13; radical change of state, 118; sting of, xv

death penalty, xix; detachment, xvi, xviii, 60
devil, 4, 16, 18, 19, 24, 60, 83, 116
Devils, The, xiv
Dostoevsky, Fyodor, xiv, xvi
dying. Art of, xv, xvi, xvii, xix, 109; as witness to love, xix, 60; consolations in, xix; dying to self, xix, xx; for Christ's sake, 61; training in, ix, xix

emotions, xviii, 81
endurance, 57
Elijah, 128
Eliot, T. S., xiv, xvi
Elisha, 128
eternity, 115
Eucharist, 131
Eusebius of Caesarea, 15
evangelization, 132
Extreme Unction, 74

faith, xix, 1, 61, 62, 67, 69, 130
forgiveness of sins, 50, 68, 110, 112, 120
fortitude, 55–57, 60
frailty, 92
Francis de Sales, St., xix, 103–6

Garden of Gethsemane, xvi, xviii, 79–87
Germanicus, 8
gift, xv
glory, 97–99
God, xv, xvi; foreknowledge of, 86; Furnace of Love, 131; goodness of, 92–93, 97, 105–6; gratitude to, 111; law of love, 127; mercy of, 4, 7, 37, 48–50, 68–69, 120–21; presence of, 96–101; remembers the dead, 121; sufficient for us, 106; union with, xviii, xix, 2; will of, 76, 103–6

God the Father, 2, 4, 68
Gospel of Matthew, xvi
grace, 86, 93, 96–97, 105, 113, 125
Gregory the Great, Pope, 57, 59
grief, xiii, xviii, xix, 33–42, 47–48, 80–87, 104, 117

happiness, eternal, 66, 92
heaven, 78, 113, 125
hell, 66
Henry VIII, xix, 79
Holy Spirit, 12, 17, 20, 63, 89, 115
hope, 67, 69, 122
humiliation, xviii
humility, xv, 65–68
Huxley, Aldous, xi

Ignatius of Antioch, St., xvii, 1–5; martyrdom of, 2
Ignatius of Loyola, St., 111, 113
Isaiah, 95

Jane de Chantal, St., xix, 103–6
Jerome, St., 59, 62
Jesus Christ, xv, 2, 31, 49, 63; agony in the Garden, 79–87; Bread of God, 4; Bridegroom of souls, 95; compassion of, 20, 85, 132; Cross of, xix, 67, 106; divinity of, 80, 85; endurance of, 4; "Eternal Eagle," 131; "folly" of, 131; friendship with, 129; image of, xv, 101; imitation of, xvi, xvii, xviii, 2, 3, 34, 86–87, 111; humility of, 67; Light of souls, 130–31; love of, xv, 1, 67, 95; obedience of, 59; Resurrection of, xv; saving work of, 121; Second Coming of, 122; self-giving death of, xv, 34, 50, 55, 131; sorrow of, 80–87; true humanity of, 85; union with, 125; weeping of, xvi

Joan of Arc, 126
John, St., 79–80
John Bosco, St., 109
John of the Cross, St., xix, 95–101
Johnson, Samuel, ix
John the Baptist, St., 62
Joseph, St., 111, 113
joy, 73–76, 93, 96, 122, 130
judgment, final, 118, 120, 122
just war, 62

Karamazov, Alyosha, xvi
Kirilov, xiv
Kübler-Ross, Elisabeth, xiii

Last Gentleman, The, xi
Lazarus, xvi, 70
Liguori, Alphonsus, St., 111, 113

Malthusian belts, xii
Manoah, 99
Marcellus, Pope, 60
martyrdom, xvi, xvii, xviii, 2–5, 7–13, 16–25, 53–63, 81–82, 86–87, 126; eagerness to suffer, 81; fear of death, 84; voluntary, 61; witness to Christ, 62
Martyrs of Gaul, xvii, xviii, 16–25
Mary Magdalene, 126
Maturus, 18, 21
Maximus, St., 55, 60
Monica, St., xviii, 43–51
More, Thomas, St., xix, 79, 89–93
Moses, 97–98
Mother Teresa, x
mourning, xviii, xix, 33–42
Muggeridge, Malcolm, x

Newman, John Henry, xix, 115
Nouwen, Henri, xv
Nuland, Sherwin, xiii

Ostia, 44

pain, 46, 73–78, 82
patience, 106
Paul, St., xx, 3, 83–84, 98, 126–27
Percy, Walker, xi
persecution, 82
Peter, St., xvii, 3, 79–80, 92
Phaedo, ix
Polycarp of Smyrna, St., xvii, 7–14; martyrdom of, 9–13
Pothinus, 20
poverty, xviii, 65–71
Purgatory, 112
prayer, xix, 9, 92–93, 104, 122
priest, xi, 109, 112, 125
Providence, 69, 71, 82, 110; self-surrender to, xix, 92, 103–6
purgation, xvi

Quintus, 9

Rasselas, ix
resurrection, xv, 2–3
Roper, Margaret, xix, 89–93

sacrifice, xv, 2, 12, 42, 110, 112–13, 128
salvation, 116, 122
Sanctus, 18, 21
Satyrus, 33–42
self-giving, xv, xvi, xix, 71
selfishness, xv, 69–70
Serapion, 30
simplicity, xviii, 106
Socrates, ix
Solomon, King, 115
sorrow, xix, 38, 47
Spiritual Combat, 106
Steiner, George, xiv
Stoics, 33
suffering, 95, 128
suicide, xiv

tears, 36, 40, 47, 49
Teresa of Avila, St., 95
terror, 86
Therese of Lisieux, St., xix, 123–32; like a bird, 129–30; "little way," 123; vocation of love, 125–32
Thomas Aquinas, St., xviii, 53–63
trust, xix, 70, 83, 93

Vettius Epagathus, 16
Virgin Mary, 111, 113, 124
vision of God, 98–101

wisdom, 44–45, 82

Zechariah, 95

About the Editor

Matthew Levering teaches theology at Ave Maria University in Naples, Florida. He is the author of several books including *On the Priesthood* (Rowman & Littlefield, 2003), *Holy People, Holy Land: A Theological Introduction to the Bible* (forthcoming, co-authored with Michael Dauphinais), *Christ's Fulfillment of Torah and Temple*, *Knowing the Love of Christ: An Introduction to the Theology of St. Thomas Aquinas* (co-authored with Michael Dauphinais), and *Scripture and Metaphysics: Aquinas and the Renewal of Trinitarian Theology*.